Chartres

The Disconnected Zodiac

RICHARD J LEGAULT

Copyright © 2021 by Richard J Legault

All rights reserved. No part of this book shall be reproduced or transmitted in any form or by any means, electronic, mechanical, magnetic, photographic including photocopying, recording or by any information storage and retrieval system, without prior written permission of the author.

AMAZON DIGITAL SERVICES, INC. 2021

410 TERRY AVENUE NORTH SEATTLE, WA 98109 UNITED STATES

ISBN: 9798516384172

Chartres - The Disconnected Zodiac

TABLE OF CONTENTS

TABLE OF CONTENTS i

SUMMARY 1

1. INTRODUCTION 3
   The Signs and Months in the Royal Portal Zodiac Sculptures 3
   The Signs and Months in the Zodiac Window 9
   Flow of Time 12
   Scope and Objective 12

2. SOCIAL AND CULTURAL CONTEXT 13
   The Months 13
   The Signs 13
   Deliberate Decision 15
   12th Century Cultural Context 15
   Plato, Ptolemy and Arabic Astronomers 16
   Medieval Cosmos and Zodiac 16
   The Shape and Motion of the Heavens 17
   Christian Concept of Time 18

3. HISTORIOGRAPHY 21
   Historiography of the Royal Portal Zodiac Anomalies 21

4. EXPLORING FASSLER'S VIEW 22
   The Feast Days 22
   Pairing of Signs and Months 23
   The Entry Method 24
   The Duration Method 27
   The Pisces Sculpture 28
   The Gemini Sculpture 30
   Baptism as Shield 30
   Heraldic Insignia of Navarre and Blois 31
   The Wisdom of the Navarrese Gemini/Jiménez 32
   Selection of Pisces and Gemini 33
   Fassler's View Assessed 33

5. MORE CONTEXT AND A NEW HYPOTHESIS 35
   Wisdom and Science in the Symbols 35

Chartres - The Disconnected Zodiac

    Hypothesis 36
    Year of Creation 37
    Bi-directional Reading 37
    Measuring Time 38
    Medieval Astronomy at Chartres 38
    Modern Precession 38
    Medieval Precession 40
    Al-Battani at Chartres 40
    Dating Creation Using Precession 41
    Armillary Sphere and Astrolabe 42
    More on Precession 45
    Challenging the Hypothesis 47
    Testability 48
    Calendar Reform and Precession 48
    Copernicus, Al-Battani and Precession 50
    Evidence and Hypothesis Assessed 51

6.   BACK TO THE WINDOW 53

    The Gemini-Taurus Transposition 53
    Proof and Understanding 56
    The Mathesis Connection 56

REFERENCES 59

NOTES 63

Chartres - The Disconnected Zodiac

SUMMARY

The signs of the zodiac (Signs) paired with the labours of the months (Months) are common in medieval art. Countless variations appear in sculpture, illuminated manuscripts and stained glass. A clear understanding of the oddities of two particular variations at Chartres Cathedral has long been elusive and problematic. The variation in the Royal Portal sculptures and another in the Zodiac Window are peculiar for two reasons. First, the sculptures are bi-directional in their calendrical sequencing with a disconnected placement of Gemini and Pisces. Second, the otherwise conventional calendrical sequence in the window transposes the placement of the May/Gemini pair with the April/Taurus pair.

Considering that the sculpture and the glass both have an anomalous treatment of Gemini, this redundancy may be approached as a deliberate design decision made with the intention of conveying specific deeper meaning that would otherwise not have been possible. The hypothesis is that it may be understood as a visual metaphor intended to represent a biblically estimated duration of the *Old Testament* period.

KEYWORDS: *Astronomy, Biblical Chronology, Cathedral Chartres, Cosmology, Gemini, Gothic, Medieval, Precession, Royal Portal, Signs and Months, Pisces, Stained Glass, Timekeeping, Zodiac.*

Chartres - The Disconnected Zodiac

1. INTRODUCTION

The Signs and Months in the Royal Portal Zodiac Sculptures

As seen in Figure 1, Pisces and Gemini are notably missing from the Signs and Months sculptures in the archivolts over the Left Door of the Royal Portal of Chartres Cathedral, *circa* 1145. Oddly, as seen in Figure 2, these two Signs appear instead over the Right Door of the Royal Portal, among images that sanctify Wisdom and the Seven Liberal Arts. I call this oddity the *Disconnected Zodiac.*

Over the Left Door each Sign is placed above its corresponding Month. There are 12 Months but only 10 Signs. The Sign-Month pairings follow the Duration method, explained in Chapter 4. The calendrical sequencing of the Signs and Months is an elaborate arrangement of the images in four seasonal groups. Each season starts at the bottom of an archivolt and ends at the top. Thus, while time flows conventionally from bottom to top, it does so in a bi-directional manner: clockwise on the left and counter clockwise on the right. Moreover, the arrangement of the seasons is such that time flows from right to left, a reversal of the more typical flow from left to right.

Figure 3 shows a table and a sketch of this highly anomalous arrangement, including blank spaces in the positions of the table where one can situate, by elimination, the places where the disconnected Pisces and Gemini should go. It is worth studying this figure to understand the highly idiosyncratic ordering of the Signs and Months, including the unusual directions of the flow of time.

The Pisces-Gemini anomaly in the sculptures is threefold. First, instead of appearing within the main group of Signs, Pisces and Gemini appear over a separate door, among images that sanctify Wisdom and the Seven Liberal Arts. Second, unlike the other ten Signs, there is no pairing of Pisces and Gemini with their respective Months. Thirdly, not only are they omitted from the seasonal groupings, they are cut one above the other into a single stone, as if they were intentionally meant to be placed together instead of paired with their Months and as if they were meant to somehow stand as a season of their own.

Figure 4 and Figure 5 are close-ups of the Signs and Months. Figure 6 is an indexed map of the all the images over the left and right doors of the Royal Portal with descriptions mainly following Etienne Houvet.[1]

Chartres - The Disconnected Zodiac

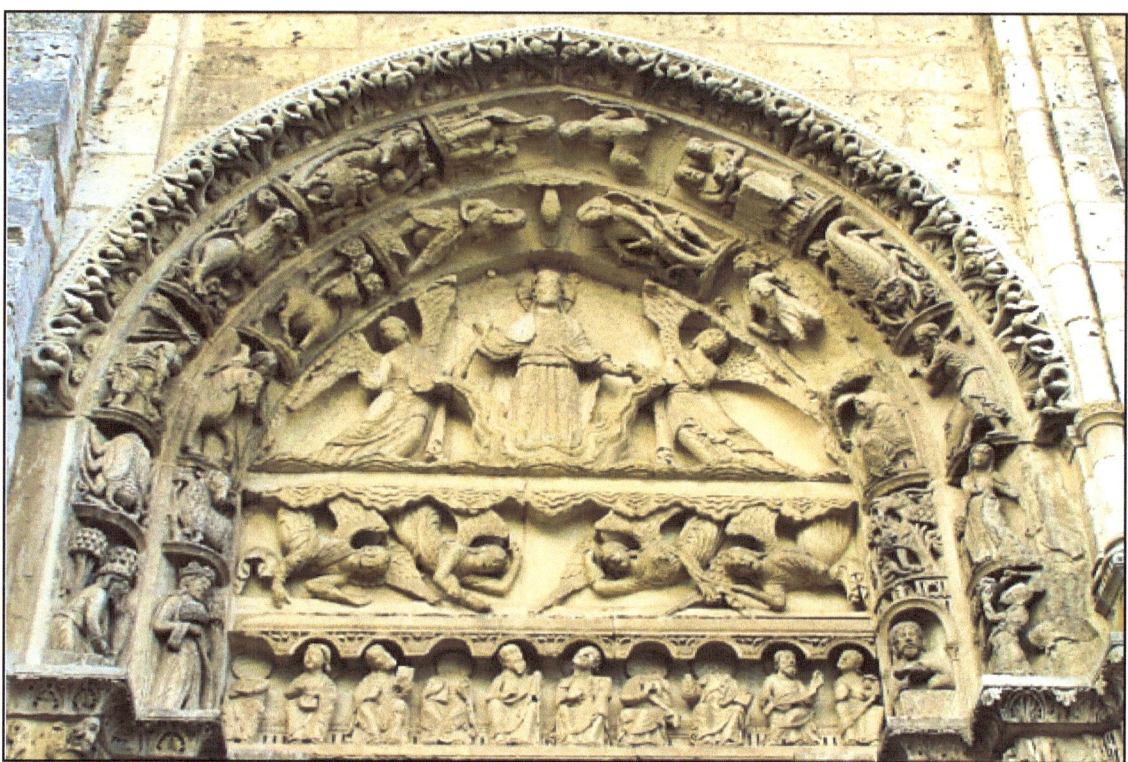

Figure 1 – The Signs and Months Sculptures in the archivolts over the Left Door of the Royal Portal of Chartres Cathedral, *circa* 1145. Image: Legault.

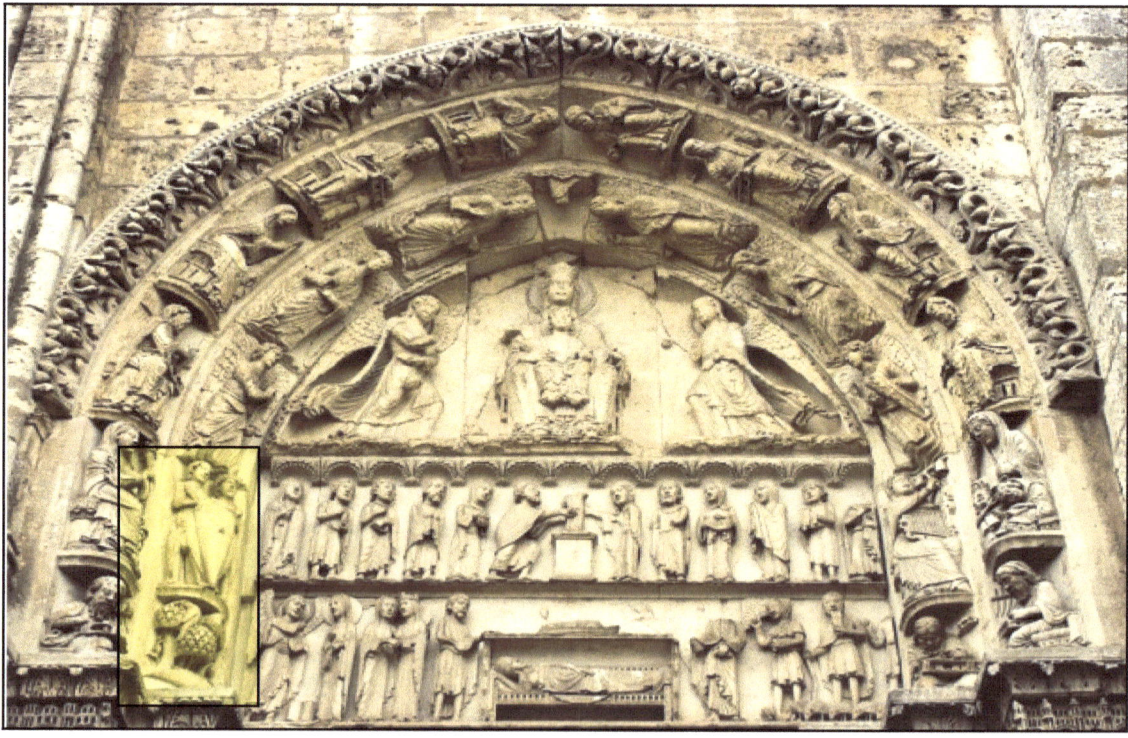

Figure 2– The Disconnected Gemini and Pisces (highlighted), placed with depictions of Wisdom and the Seven Liberal Arts, in the archivolts above the Right Door of the Royal Portal of Chartres Cathedral, *circa* 1145. Image: Legault.

Chartres - The Disconnected Zodiac

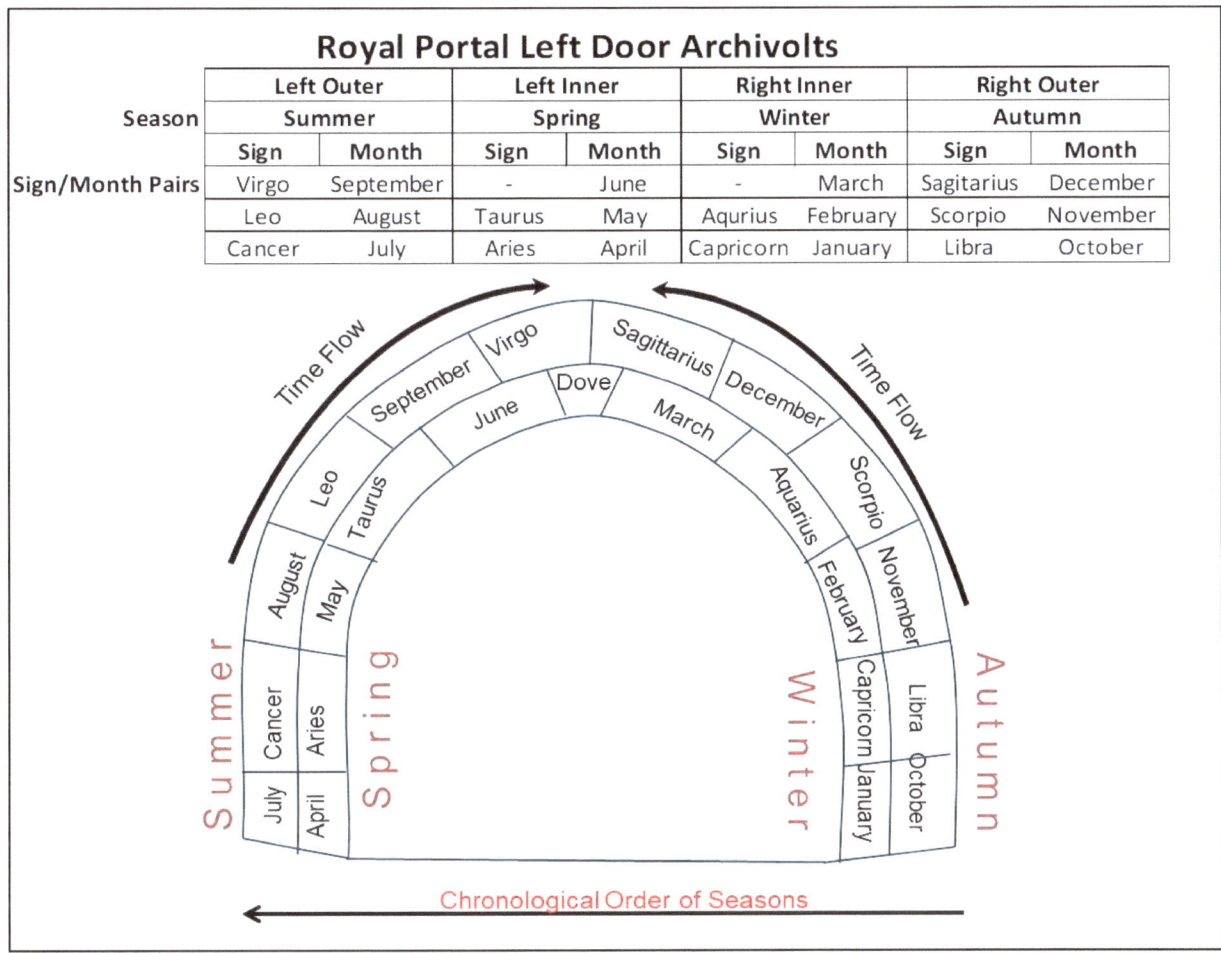

Figure 3 - Table and Diagram of the anomalous chronological order of the paired Signs/Months, grouped by Season, over the left door of the Royal Portal. The two blanks spaces in the table show where Pisces and Gemini ought to go. Image: Legault.

Chartres - The Disconnected Zodiac

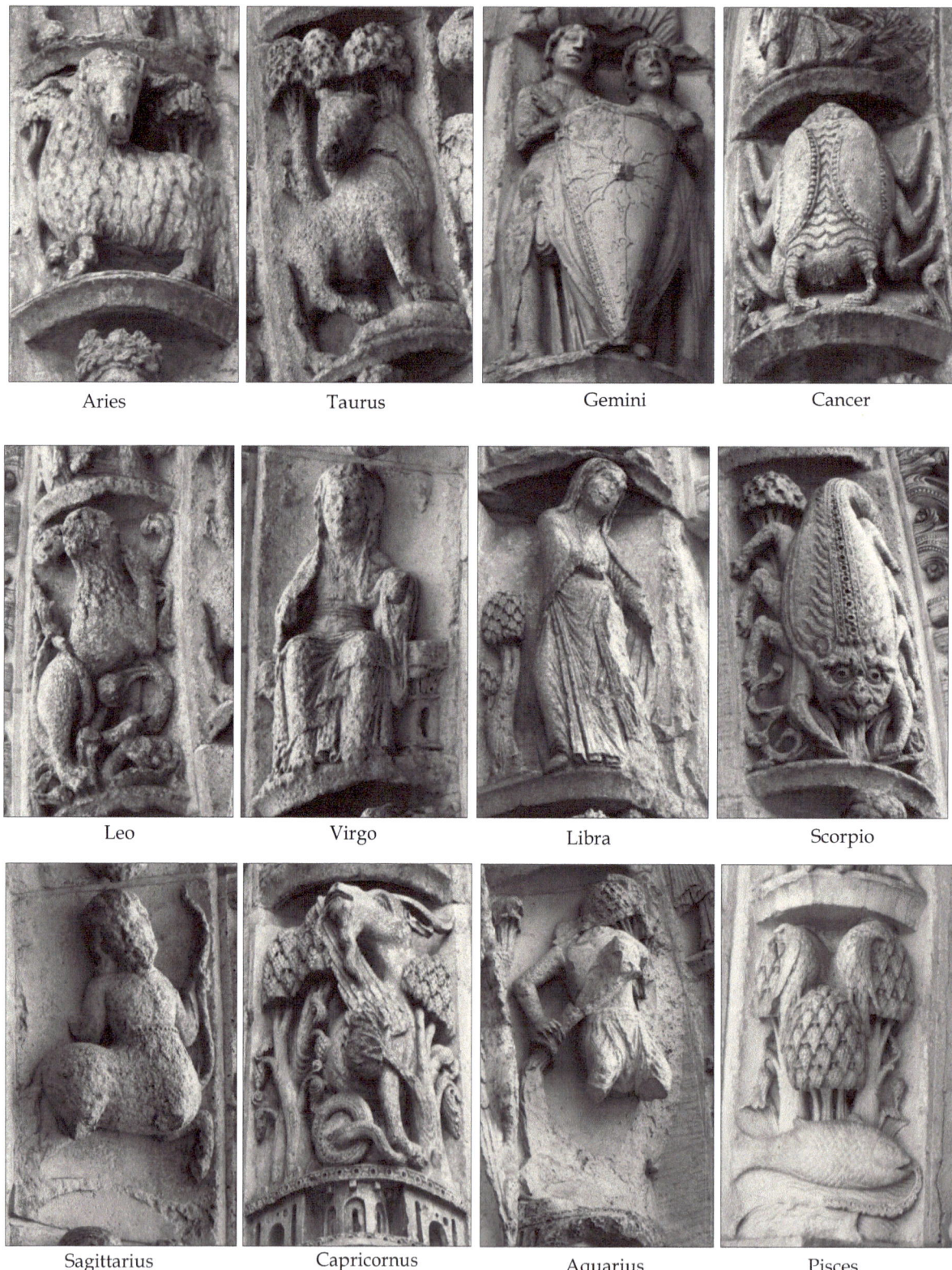

Figure 4 - Zodiac Signs in the archivolts of the Royal Portal *ca.* 1145. Images: Chris Henige see: http://www.fabricae.org/V8/Shared/PHP/Portal.php?proj=P&id=CHARTRES&pid=WL

Chartres - The Disconnected Zodiac

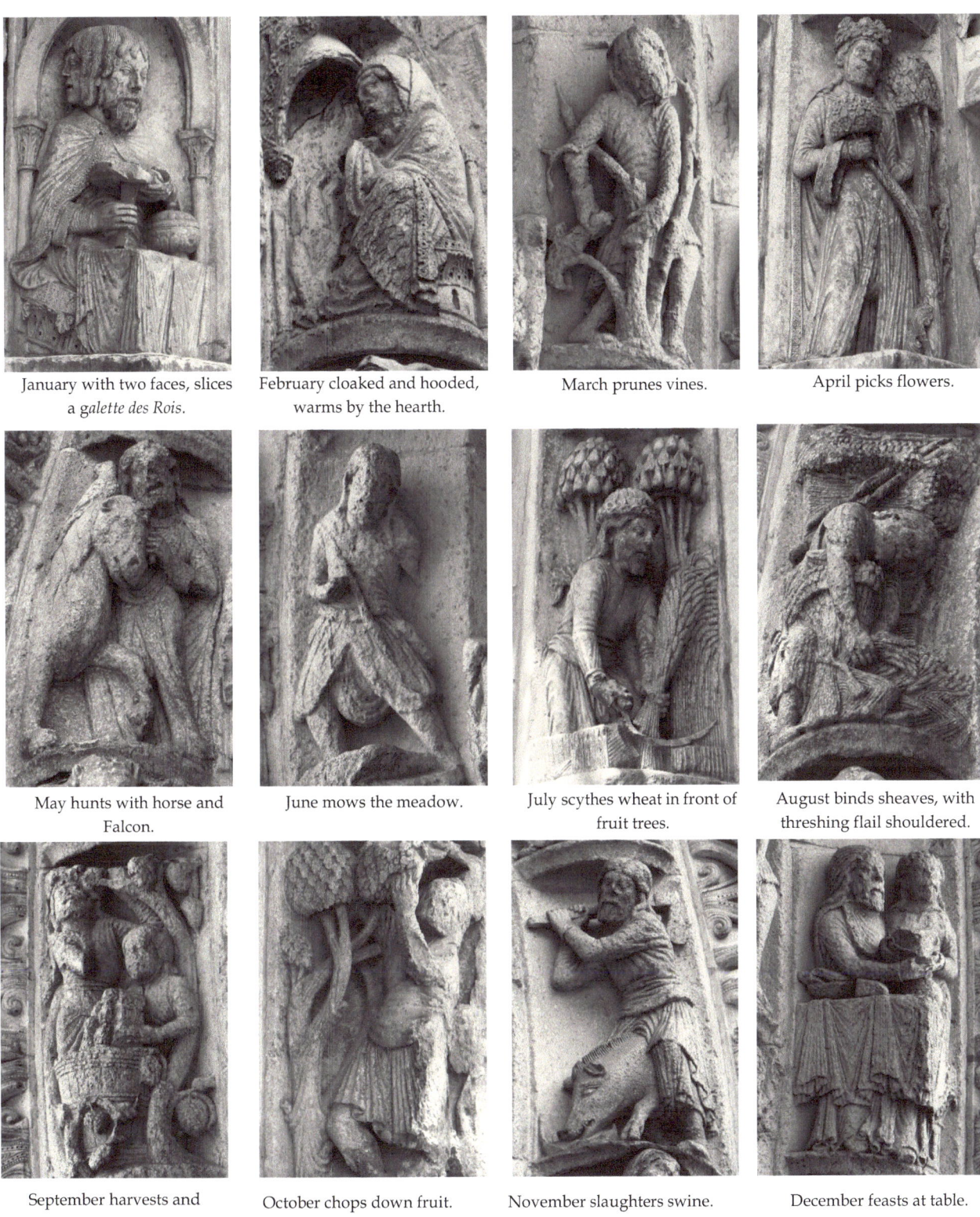

January with two faces, slices a *galette des Rois*.

February cloaked and hooded, warms by the hearth.

March prunes vines.

April picks flowers.

May hunts with horse and Falcon.

June mows the meadow.

July scythes wheat in front of fruit trees.

August binds sheaves, with threshing flail shouldered.

September harvests and presses grapes.

October chops down fruit.

November slaughters swine.

December feasts at table.

Figure 5 - Labours of the Months in the archivolts of the Royal Portal, *ca* 1145. Images: Chris Henige see: http://www.fabricae.org/V8/Shared/PHP/Portal.php?proj=P&id=CHARTRES&pid=WL

Chartres - The Disconnected Zodiac

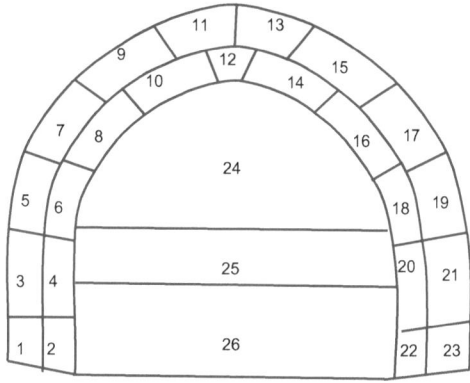
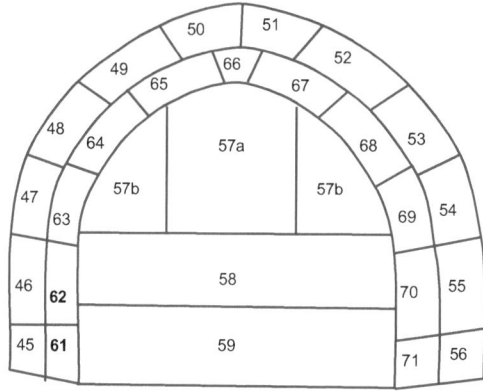

Left Door

1. July Harvest of Wheat.
2. April Pruning Trees Picking Flowers.
3. Cancer 21 Jun - 22 July
4. Aires 21 Mar - 19 April
5. August Binding Sheaves and Threshing
6. May Hunting/Falconry
7. Leo 23 July - 22 Aug
8. Taurus 20 April - 20 May
9. September Harvest and Pressing of Grapes
10. June Hoeing, Mowing
11. Virgo 23 Aug - 22 Sept
12. Mutilaed Dove Holy Spirit, cruciform nimbus
13. Sagittarius 22 Nov - 21 Dec
14. March Pruning Vines
15. December Couple at Table Feasting
16. Aquarius 20 Jan - 18 Feb
17. Scorpio 23 Oct - 21 Nov
18. February - Keeping warm by the Hearth
19. November Slaughtering Swine
20. Capricorn 22 Dec - 19 Jan
21. Libra 23 Sept - 22 Oct
22. January (Two Faced Janus) Feasting
23. October Chopping down Fruit
24. God in a V-shaped cloud
25. Four Angels
26. Seated Ten, necks craned, with scrolls and books

Right Door

45. Aristotle (Dialectic)
46. Dialectic - Personified
47. Cicero (Rhetoric)
48. Rhetoric - Personified
49. Euclid (Geometry)
50. Geometry - Personified
51. Arithmetic Personified
52. Boethius (Arithmentic)
53. Astronomy - Personfied
54. Ptolemy (Astronomy)
55. Grammar - Personified
56. Priscian or Donato Grammar
57a. Holy Virgin with Christ Child
57b. Two angels with censors (damaged)
58. Presentation of Jesus at the Temple.
59. Annunciation, Visitation and Nativity
61. **Pisces**
62. **Gemini**
63 - 65. Angels with Censor
66. Mutilaed: Hand of God?
67-69. Angels with Censor
70. Music - Personified
71. Pythagoras (Music)

Figure 6 – Map and Legend of the Sculptures over the Left and Right Doors of the Royal Portal with the Signs and Months images highlighted in Bold.

Chartres - The Disconnected Zodiac

The Signs and Months in the Zodiac Window

The Zodiac Window of Chartres Cathedral, *circa* 1217, is shown in Figure 7. The calendrical sequence starts at the bottom with January (Three Faced Man) paired with Aquarius. It ends at the top with December (Feasting) paired with Capricorn, just below a Christ enthroned in Majesty.

Chartres Cathedral Zodiac Window

27 Christ *Chronocrator*, Alpha, Omega, Burning Candles
26 Capricornus
25 December Feasting
24 Sagitarius
23 November - Slaughtering Pig (The pane is actually labelled December)
22 October/Scorpio - Pouring Wine
21 Libra
20 September - Wine Making
19 Virgo
18 August - Threshing Grain
17 July/Leo - Harvesting Grain
16 Cancer
15 June - Mowing
14 May/Gemini - Hunting?
13 Taurus
12 April - Flowers
11 Aries
10 March - Pruning Vines
9 Pisces
8 February - Warning before a Hearth
7 January/Aquarius - Three Faces
6 Donors - Vintners
5 Donors - Vintners
4 Donors - Vintners
3 Bell Ringer
2 Donor: Count Theobald
1 Donors - Vintners

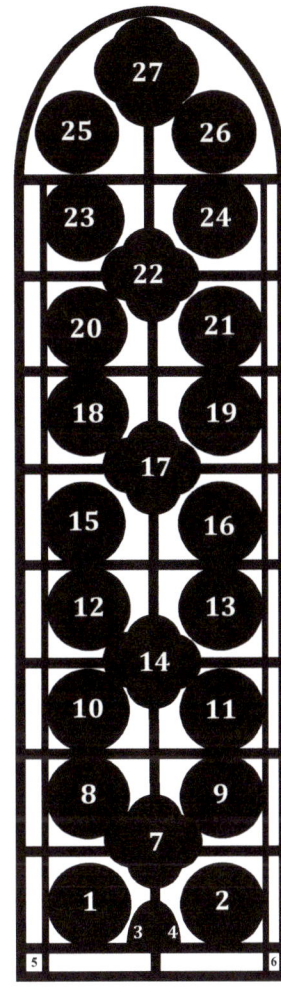
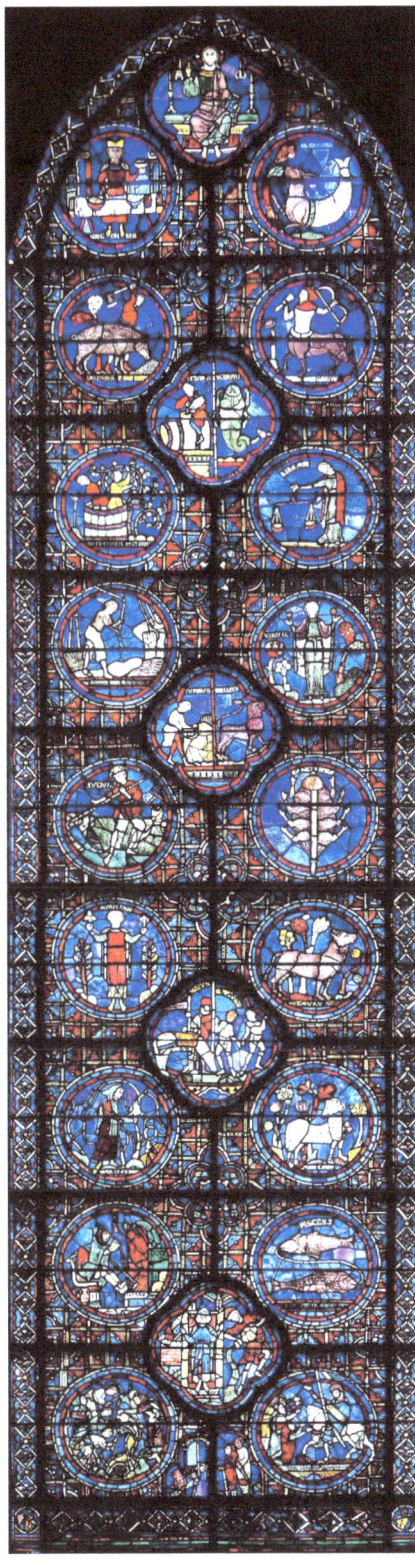

Figure 7 - Chartres Zodiac Window (*ca.* 1217) - Christ (*Chronocrator*) sits at the top flanked by the Alpha and Omega. Time runs from the bottom up. The Labours of the Months and Signs of the Zodiac are paired using the Entry Method and in calendrical order, except that April/Gemini is transposed with May/Taurus. At the bottom are the donors: Thibault VI count of Chartres, on behalf of Thomas count of Perche, and Vintners.
Images:
Legend diagram: Legault
Descriptions adapted from: Jane Vadnal and Alison Stones:
https://www.medart.pitt.edu/image/France/Chartres/Chartres-Cathedral/Windows/Choir-windows/028A-Zodiac/chartres-028AZodiac-main.html
Window: Public domain:
https://upload.wikimedia.org/wikipedia/commons/c/ca/Chartres-028-g_composite.jpg

Chartres - The Disconnected Zodiac

Christ Lord of Time – At the top of the Zodiac Window sits an enthroned Christ. The throne emphasises his leadership role as all powerful Lord, creator and ruler of heaven and earth. The Greeks called it: Christ *Pantocrator*. When flanked by the Alpha and Omega and placed above or outside a zodiac cycle, Christ's all-powerful lordship over time is emphasised and sometimes called Christ *Chronocrator*.

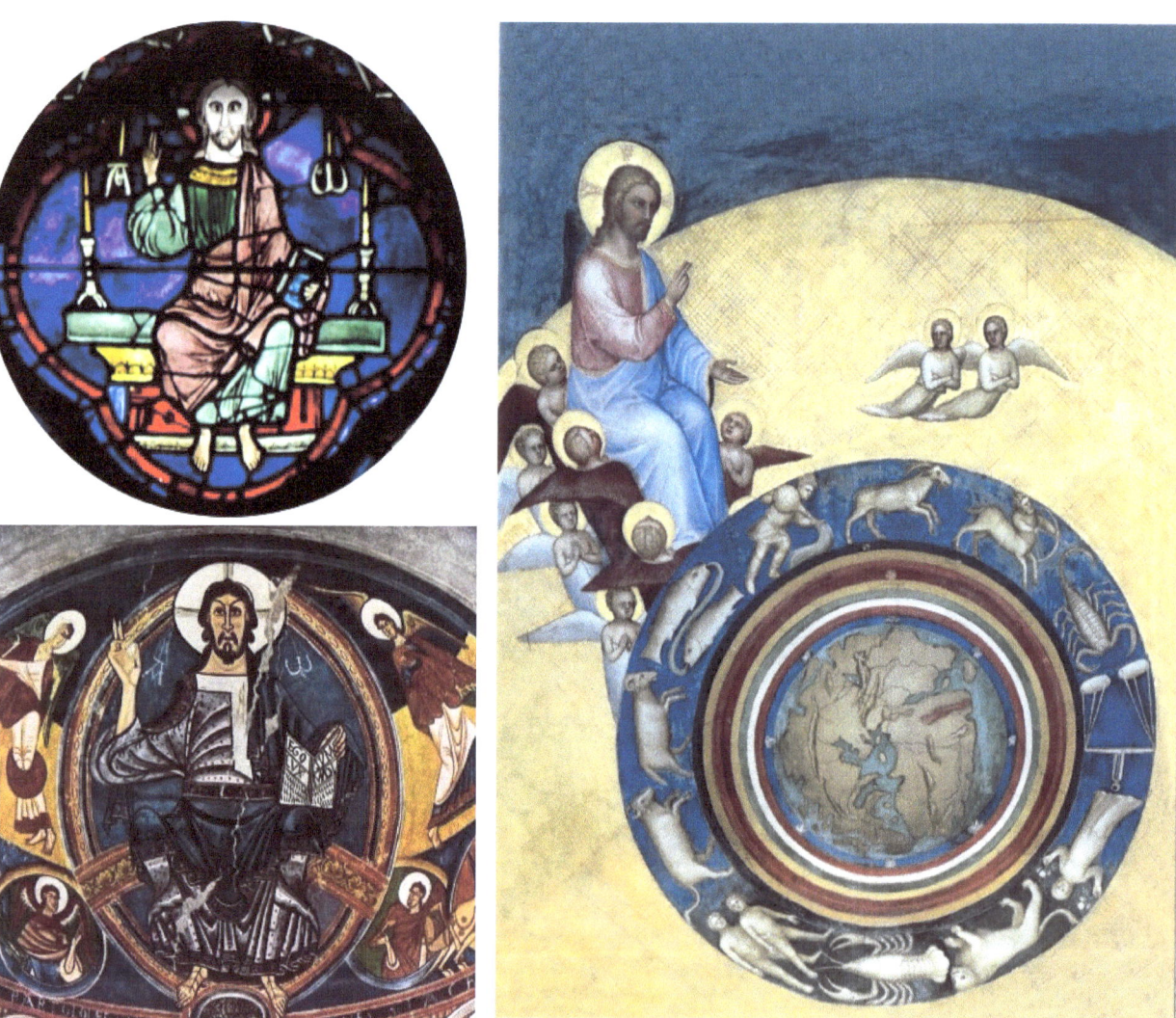

Figure 8 - Christ Lord of Time (*Chronocrator*)

Top Left: Christ in Majesty flanked by burning candles and the Alpha and Omega, Chartres Zodiac Window, *ca.* 1145   https://commons.wikimedia.org/wiki/File:Chartres-028-g_-_alpha_omega.jpg

Bottom Left: Christ *Pantocrator* in mandorla and flanked by Alpha and Omega, **S**ant Climent de Taüll, Catalonia, *ca.* 1123
https://upload.wikimedia.org/wikipedia/commons/e/ed/Meister_aus_Tahull_001.jpg

Right: Creation - Christ *Pantocrator* initiates and governs the motions of the Cosmos and the flow of time, by Giusto de' Menabuoi, Padua, *ca.* 1377,
https://en.wikipedia.org/wiki/Padua_Baptistery#/media/File:Battistero_5_--.jpg

Chartres - The Disconnected Zodiac

The first and last letters of the Greek alphabet, *Alpha* (A, α) and *Omega* (Ω, ω) are direct references to *Revelation* 1:8 "I am Alpha and Omega, the beginning and the ending, saith the Lord, which is, and which was, and which is to come, the Almighty." A mandorla in such an image, represents more than just a full body nimbus, it must be understood as a portal through which the all-powerful Lord transits between earthly time and celestial eternity. These aspects or attributes of Christ are emphasised in the images in Figure 8. The addition of burning candles in the Chartres Zodiac Window further emphasises rulership over the ongoing passage of earthly time. The placement of the enthroned Christ between the Alpha and Omega points of finite earthly time, also remind us that Christ came into the world, in the flesh, as the Word or Wisdom Incarnate at an intermediate moment in finite time, a pivotal moment situated in between the Alpha and Omega points.

Accordingly, the attributes of Christ at the top of the Zodiac window identify him as the Lord who rules over both celestial eternity and earthly time. The image is very much one of Christ as *Chronocrator*, the all-powerful ruler who not only sets time in motion but governs its every passing moment, day by day, month by month, year by year, from the beginning to the end. At the same time it is an image that situates the coming of Christ into the world at an intermediate point between the Alpha and Omega.

In counterpoint to the majesty of Christ at the top centre, a humble bell ringer, in the bottom centre pane of the window, seen in Figure 9, administers local earthly time by ringing out the hours of the divine office.

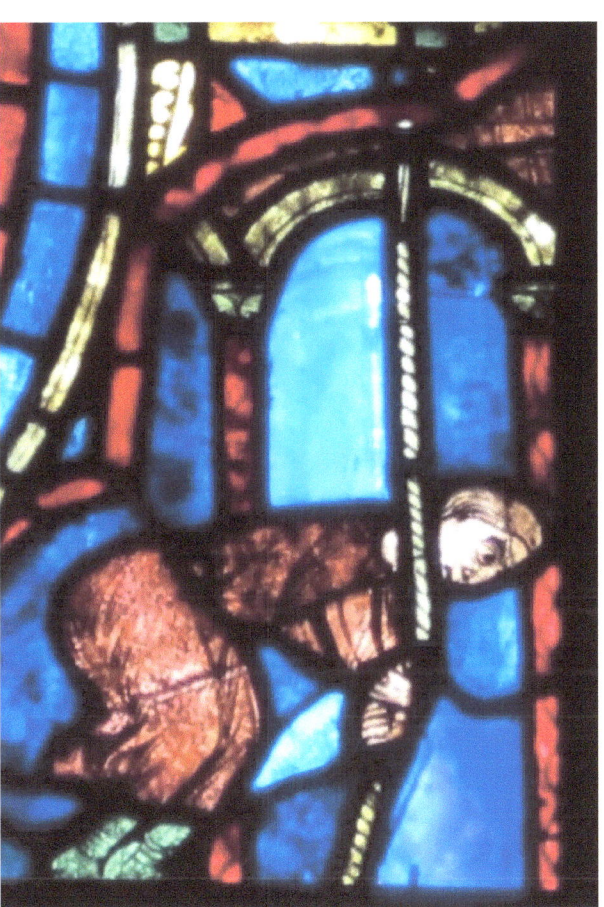

Figure 9 – A Humble Bell Ringer - Zodiac Window bottom centre pane, Chartres Cathedral *ca*. 1217.

Image: cropped from:
https://upload.wikimedia.org/wikipedia/commons/c/ca/Chartres-028-g_composite.jpg

Chartres - The Disconnected Zodiac

Flow of Time

The panes of the Zodiac Window work their way through the year in the conventional calendrical order with time flowing from the bottom up except that the May/Gemini pair is transposed with the April/Taurus pair. The indexed mapping in Figure 7 clearly shows how the May/Gemini pane in position 14 is out of sequence. Reading from the bottom up, May/Gemini in position 14 comes before, instead of after, April in position 12 and Taurus in position 13.

Scope and Objective

My objective with this booklet is limited to the details of the Disconnected Zodiac. It is focussed more narrowly on the details of the anomalous treatment of Pisces and Gemini so as to explain the deeper astronomical meaning it conveys. The much broader meaning conveyed by the full suite of images over the left door of the Royal Portal, the so called Ascension Scene, is a subject I hope to treat at greater length in a separate booklet. Here, I simply want to show how Gemini anomaly in the Zodiac Window is a redundant and secondary reaffirmation of the earlier anomalies in the sculptures. I will propose how the idea of bi-directional reading and reversal of direction, in terms of medieval astronomy, is key to a workable hypothesis explaining the reasoning behind the Disconnected Zodiac of Chartres Cathedral.

Chartres -The Disconnected Zodiac

2. SOCIAL AND CULTURAL CONTEXT

The Months

Medieval art depicts calendar cycles of monthly activities so often in stone, glass and illuminated manuscripts that historians of art have defined an iconology of medieval images known as the Labours of the Months (Months). As Colum Hourihane explains it, generally, a typical and seasonally repetitive rural activity symbolically depicts each month, for example, pruning in April, hunting and falconry in May, planting and weeding in June and so on.[2] These activities and the iconology vary a lot from place to place with different activities taking place earlier or later in the year depending on local climate, length of seasons and customs. Specific icons of the Signs and Months are easier to understand when the artists label each one with the name of the sign and the month in letters, as in the Chartres Zodiac window pane for the May(Hunting)-Gemini pair, shown close-up in Figure 24.

The Signs

Very often, as in the Royal Portal and in the Zodiac Window, the Months are paired, one for one, with the even more standardized iconology of the twelve Signs of the Zodiac (Signs), a medieval adaptation of the traditional astronomical lore of late Greek and Roman antiquity. Across all cultures, astronomy has always been essential to keep calendars on track with the natural cycles of time – the days, the months, the seasons and the years. In medieval art, the Months and the Signs usually, but by no means always, appear in the standard chronological order of calendar time. There are several examples of this at Chartres. The Zodiac Window, *circa* 1217, shown in Figure 7, apart from its treatment of Gemini, is one example. In another example in Figure 10, the archivolts of the rightmost door of the North Transept Porch of Chartres Cathedral, *circa* 1215, the direction of time runs clockwise across the archivolt, without interruption from January to December. The Signs are in the outer archivolt and the Months are on the inner one – all in the normal and uninterrupted calendrical sequence and with side-by-side pairings following the Duration method. In the much later Chartres Zodiacal Clock, *circa* 1525, in Figure 11 the Signs of the Zodiac run in conventional calendric order counter-clockwise while the hours of the day run clockwise. The clock shows the phases of the Moon but not the Months.

Chartres - The Disconnected Zodiac

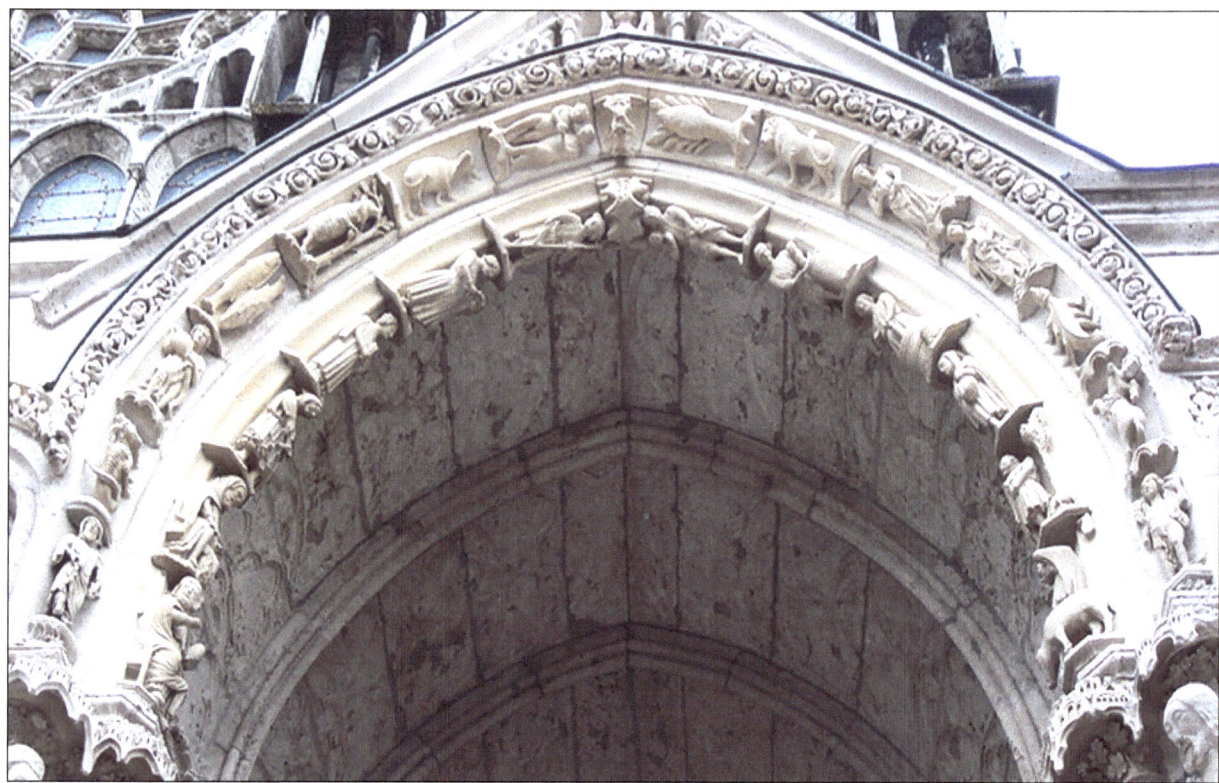

Figure 10- Chartres North Porch Zodiac -The Signs and the Months in the archivolts of the North Porch run clockwise from January on the left through June at the top to December on the right. The two extra figures at each end depict winter and summer: men in seasonally appropriate attire (*ca.* 1215 – restored). The Signs and the Months are paired side by side, using the Duration Method. Image: Chris Henige.

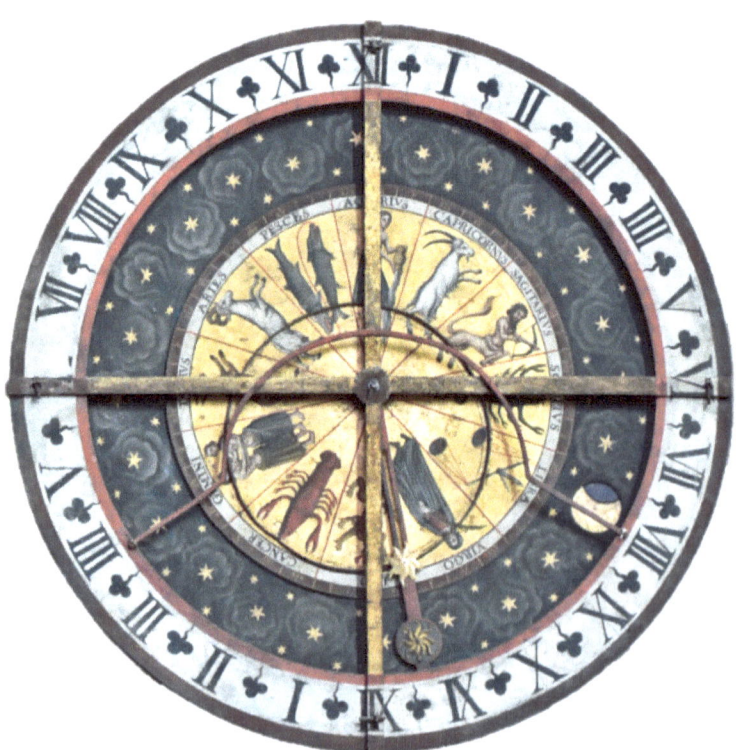

Figure 11 - The Zodiacal Clock at Chartres - The flow of time for the Signs runs counter clockwise in proper calendrical sequence. The flow of time for the hours runs clockwise. The Sun is just past the 11th hour of the morning of 22 or 23 August, on the cusp between Leo and Virgo and the Moon is about ¾ full in Libra (*ca.* 1525-28). Image Steve Pseno, Pinterest, see:
https://i.pinimg.com/originals/5d/5f/86/5d5f8617ddf8bfbce831196f72a745d8.jpg

Chartres - The Disconnected Zodiac

Deliberate Decision

The archivolt sculptures of the Royal Portal anomalously place a disconnected Pisces and Gemini over a different door in among images of Wisdom and the Seven Liberal Arts. The Zodiac Window transposes the May/Gemini pair with the April/Taurus pair. I can understand these two anomalies, both involving Gemini, neither as an error on the part of the original artists nor as botched restorations. I think there can be no question that ignorance or error is the cause of the disconnected Zodiac. Nor can they be the cause of the odd transposition in the Zodiac window. The correct chronological order of the Signs was common knowledge to 12th Century medieval culture. Their cosmology, astronomy and time reckoning methods, inherited from classical Greek and Roman teachings, were available in the Latin works of medieval natural philosophers such as Beothius, the Venerable Bede, Isidore of Seville, Abbo of Fleury and numerous others. The exceptional interest in and knowledge of astronomy among the medieval Chartrians, from the days of Bishop Fulbert of Chartres (*ca.* 1006) up to the chancellorship of Thierry of Chartres (*ca.* 1145) is a well-documented fact of history.[3] Accordingly, I think that these two anomalies in the Royal Portal and the Zodiac Window are a matter of deliberate decision. Considering the highly conservative mentality of the middle ages, I think it is reasonable to consider that when medieval artists make a deliberate choice to depart from long accepted tradition and convention, it is because they have something unconventional to say. The artists and decision makers, alas, left no written record of the reasoning behind their choices, no record of the teaching they intended to convey with these two anomalous designs. We do not even know for sure who they were.

It is up to us to let the artwork speak with its own voice.

12th Century Cultural Context

We have considerable and reasonably reliable knowledge of the cultural context of medieval Christian theology, natural philosophy, cosmology and astronomy that were read about, written about and taught in the twelfth century Chartrian community at their cathedral school. If we accept the idea that their cathedral is a stone and glass record of their teachings, then I think the best way to understand the meaning of their Zodiac anomalies is to look for clues in the Chartrian readings, writings and teachings of which the stone and glass version is a legible duplicate. Extracting and explaining the deeper meaning of the Zodiac anomalies of Chartres Cathedral in this way is the goal of this booklet.

Chartres - The Disconnected Zodiac

Plato, Ptolemy and Arabic Astronomers

At the time the Chartrians built the Royal Portal (*ca.* 1145), their astronomy and the structure of their cosmos followed the teachings of Plato, Claudius Ptolemy and Arabic astronomers. Up to that time, for Plato they had only had the 4th Century incomplete Latin translation by Calcidius of the *Timaeus* and for Ptolemy, only second and third hand summaries, compilations and commentaries from other authors of late antiquity. Ptolemy's actual books, however, were just beginning to become available, arriving in Latin translations from Arabic versions during this period of the twelfth century: the *Tetrabiblos, ca.*1138, from Plato de Tivoli, the *Planisphere, ca.*1143, from Hermann of Carinthia, and the *Almagest, ca.* 1175 from Gerard of Cremona. As we will see, there is also good evidence the Chartrians had some of the most up-to-date and more accurate astronomical teachings of the medieval Arabic astronomers Al-Kwarizmi (died: 850 AD) and Al-Battani (died: 929 AD).

Medieval Cosmos and Zodiac

The stately east-to-west pageant of the fixed stars, including the constellations of the Zodiac, across the sky each night was common knowledge to medieval philosophers and astronomers. The name Zodiac adopted into Latin came from the Greek *zōdiakos kuklos* (ζοδιακος κὐκλος), meaning 'circle of animals.' They understood these stars as fixed, never moving with respect to each other. Perhaps the longest lasting game of connect-the-dots of all time, the idea of the Zodiac and its constellations is still, to this very day, a convenient sky mapping and memory tool. Back then, as for today, astronomers defined the Zodiac as a 360 degree circular band or belt around the sphere of the sky. In antiquity and medieval times, astronomers defined the width of the Zodiac as the boundaries within which the wanderings of naked eye planets all took place and beyond which they never strayed. The width of the belt was refined over the centuries as observation techniques improved. Geminus of Rhodes in the first century, for example, sized it at 12 degrees wide, which is 6 degrees above and 6 degrees below the ecliptic circle.[4] Today the modern value, based on more precise measurement of the amount of inclination of planetary orbits, is usually given as 16 degrees.[5]

The centre of the Zodiac running 360 degrees lengthwise is the apparent path of the Sun, then and still called the Ecliptic circle. Unknown in those times is that the Ecliptic circle is in fact the orbital path of the Earth around the Sun.

They divided the length of the circular belt of the Zodiac into 12 equal segments, each one spanning 30 degrees of celestial longitude along the Ecliptic. They thought of the fixed stars visible within each one of these 30 x 16 degree rectangles of sky as composing the twelve constellations of the Zodiac. The modern constellations that retain the names of the twelve constellations of the medieval Zodiac no longer conform to these precise boundaries. In 1930, the International Astronomical Union (IAU) redefined the official boundaries of all of the 88 standard constellations based on a new map commissioned from the astronomer Eugène Joseph Delporte.[6, 7]

The Shape and Motion of the Heavens

According to Plato and Ptolemy, the fixed stars and constellations resided on an outermost celestial sphere that carried the entire stellar panorama in an east-west direction on a daily revolution around the Earth. It was inside this outermost sphere and inside the boundaries of belt of the Zodiac that the heavenly wanderings of a few misbehaving stars could be seen. This was the motions of seven stars Plato and Ptolemy had called planets because of their wandering motion visible from night to night, month to month, and even year to year, from west to east (prograde), against the fixed background of the twelve constellations of the Zodiac. The seven planets, each one on a sphere of its own, nested one inside the other like Russian Dolls, were the Moon, Sun, Mercury, Venus, Mars, Jupiter and Saturn. This Ptolemaic Model, as we now call it, appears frequently in medieval manuscripts using diagrams of concentric circles surrounded by the signs of the zodiac, as seen in Figure 12. Such diagrams - a sort of cross-section through the spheres – need to be understood as technical drawings that helped visualize in two dimensions the concept of a three dimensional spherical cosmos.

While different planets at different times were seen to sometimes reverse direction and move backwards – East to West (retrograde) - through the Zodiac for short periods of time, in general, their movement was seen as an ongoing west-east pageant, with each planet completing its cycle through the Zodiac in its own unique period of time. These planetary time periods, especially of the Sun and the Moon, were so regular and so reliable that astronomers following Plato's *Timaeus* regarded them as the ideal keepers or guardians of time – the years, the seasons, the months and the days:

> [The Demiurge] began to think of making a moving image of eternity: at the same time as he brought order to the universe, he would make an eternal image, moving according to number, of eternity remaining in unity. This, of course, is what we call "time." … [The Demiurge] brought into being the Sun, the Moon, and five other stars, for the begetting of time. These are called "wanderers" [planêta], and they stand guard over the numbers of time. … And so people are all but ignorant of the fact that time really is the wanderings of these bodies.
> Plato, *The Timaeus* [8]

Chartres - The Disconnected Zodiac

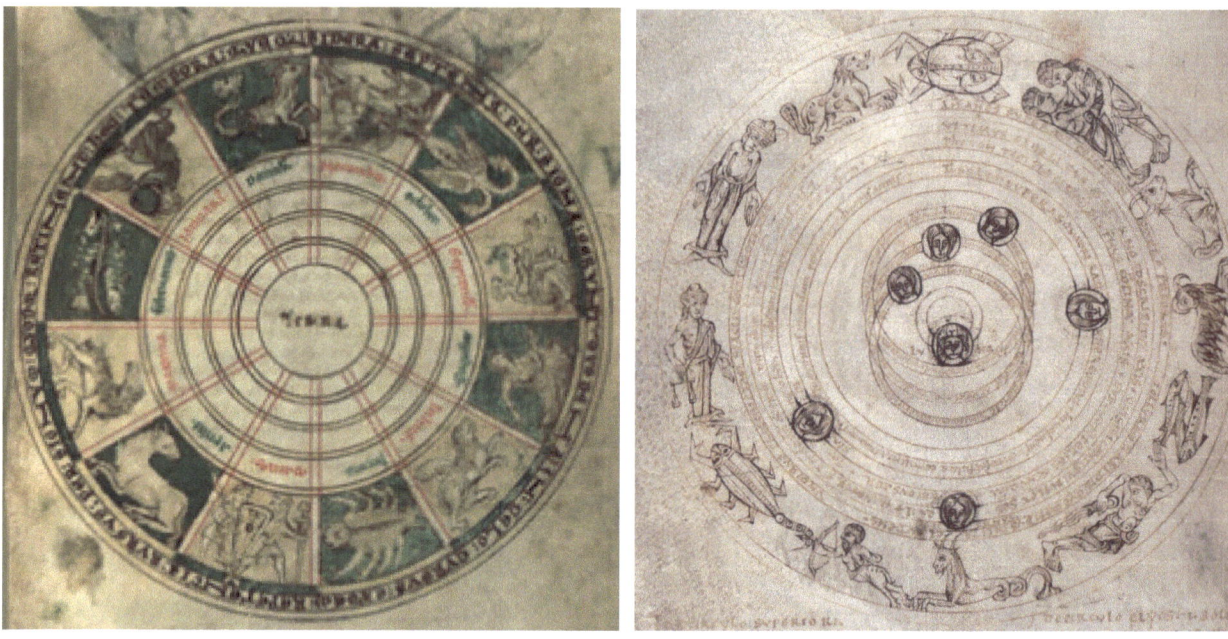

Figure 12 - Medieval Ptolemaic Diagrams

Left: From a manuscript compendium of computistical texts compiled from Bede, Isidore of Seville and Abbo of Fleury. Walters Ms. W.73, England in the late twelfth century.

Right: From the oldest scientific manuscript in the National Library of Whales, in Caroline minuscule, in two sections, the first copied c. 1000, in the Limoges area of France, probably in the milieu of Adémar de Chabannes (989-1034), the second from the same region, may be dated c. 1150.
See: https://www.thedigitalwalters.org/Data/WaltersManuscripts/W73/data/W.73/sap/W73_000003_sap.jpg
and
https://en.wikipedia.org/wiki/Zodiac#/media/File:F4.v._zodiac_circle_with_planets_-_NLW_MS_735C.png

Christian Concept of Time

While the Cosmos of Plato and Ptolemy was all very well, medieval Christians accepted its concept of repeating time cycles only as a sub-set of a much larger concept of time that remains to this day fundamental to Jewish, Muslim and Christian religious teaching. The main theological idea is that time itself is an artefact, created by God, who stands back, outside of time. According to these teachings, time begins at a moment of Creation, flows only in one direction during the history of the world and ends at an apocalyptic moment on a Day of Judgement. A core teaching of the Christian variation on this idea is that historical time, between the two end-points of Creation and Judgement Day, consists of two great periods. In the Christian view, the Incarnation - God in the flesh entering time and the created world - represents a pivotal moment in world history that separates the two great periods.

Chartres - The Disconnected Zodiac

The structure of the Christian *Bible* precisely and most fundamentally, reflects this idea, divided as it is into the *Old Testament* (the time before Christ) and the *New Testament* (the time after Christ's arrival on Earth). Like it or not, this division of historical time is still in worldwide cultural use today in the conventional Western civil calendar. Regardless of how forcefully the politically correct may gnash their teeth and decry the practice, the Western world still counts years in terms of the *Anno Domini* epoch (literally, Years of Our Lord) with year number one designated, though not without error, by Dionysius Exeguus in the 6th Century, as the birth of Christ.

The objective of medieval cathedral artwork was primarily to record and communicate cultural teachings using the medieval communication technologies of stone sculpture and stained glass images. Accordingly, it makes sense to think that their sculpture and stained glass would show, in possibly many ways, this most fundamental concept of theological time and of its three key moments. The idea, after all, is at the very core of Christian teaching. This concept of time is the one constant, the fixed framework, the ever-present backdrop upon which the complete sweep of the *Bible* narrative unfolds, from *Genesis* to *Revelation*. Some art historians think this concept of linear time is precisely the overall theme of the sculptures over the three doors of the Royal Portal of Chartres Cathedral: Creation on the left, Second Coming in the centre and the Incarnation on the right.[9]

Chartres - The Disconnected Zodiac

3. HISTORIOGRAPHY

Historiography of the Royal Portal Zodiac Anomalies

The sculptures of the Royal Portal include an anomalous arrangement of the twelve Signs of the Zodiac. Ten appear over the left door, none over the middle door and two, Gemini and Pisces, appear over the right door. After nearly a century and a half of commentary, the meaning of this anomaly has eluded many of the authors who describe it without offering any satisfactory explanation. As early as 1881, Paul Durand, commenting on a plate in his book showing scene sculpted over the left door, wrote:

> *Le sujet que nous offre cette planche est encore aujourd'hui inexpliqué. C'est une composition symbolique, dont nous n'avons pas la clef et dont nous ne connaissons pas un second exemple dans les monuments du moyen âge.*
>
> (The subject that we are offered by this plate is still today unexplained. It is a symbolic composition for which we do not have the key and of which we do not know a second example in the monuments of the middle ages.)[10]

In 1964, Adolf Katzenellenbogen wrote: "The two signs [Pisces and Gemini] pose a particular problem for which no definite solution may be offered."[11] In 1974, John James attempted an astrological explanation based on Ptolemaic esoteric mysticism the mumbo-jumbo of which, frankly, impedes a reasoned understanding.[12] In 2008, Philip Ball wrote, "We no longer know how to read this code."[13]

An outstanding exception is Margot Fassler who wrote in 2010 that Pisces and Gemini over the Incarnation doorway symbolize March and June, the months of the liturgical calendar in which fall the annual feast days of the Annunciation on 25 March and of John the Baptist on 24 June.[14] Her idea is indeed a meaningful calendrical and elegantly simple semantic fit with the rest of the Incarnation images over the right door of the Royal Portal. The Annunciation, after all, was regarded as the moment of Incarnation, the moment the Virgin Mary conceived and became pregnant by the divine intervention of the Holy Spirit. Moreover, Fassler reports that Jean Villette argued in 1994 that there once stood a trumeau statue of the Baptist in the Royal Portal.

Before proposing my own explanation, it is worthwhile to review the broader historical details and social contexts of Fassler's.

4. EXPLORING FASSLER'S VIEW

Margot Fassler's view makes two proposals. First, she proposes that the oddly placed Pisces and Gemini are symbolic of the calendar months March and June, respectively. Second, her view means that the Chartrians chose these two Signs, over all the others, to represent these months over the Incarnation door, to communicate the semantic connection between the Incarnation and the two feast days of the Annunciation on March 25 and of John the Baptist on 24 June.[15]

The Feast Days

The feast of the Annunciation commemorates the moment in the *Gospel of Luke* (1:26-38) when the Archangel Gabriel appears to the Virgin Mary and announces to her, "You will conceive and give birth to a son, and you are to call him Jesus." Medieval Christians regarded this as the moment that Mary conceived and became pregnant by divine intervention of the Holy Spirit. Since the Tenth Council of Toledo in AD 656, at the latest, Christians have recognized this moment in *Luke* as the moment of Incarnation. It is from the moment of the Annunciation that, theologically speaking, God in the flesh has made a transit from celestial eternity and entered the earthly world of historical time.

The semantic connection of the Incarnation with the June 24 feast commemorating the birth of John the Baptist also stems from the *Gospel of Luke*. It describes, in verses 1:39–56, the visit that the newly pregnant Virgin Mary makes to her relative Elizabeth (often assumed a first cousin of Mary) who is already six months pregnant with the Baptist. Christians commonly call this event the Visitation. The Visitation did not have its own feast day until the Order of the Friars Minor (the Franciscans), founded in 1206 by Francis of Assisi, began to celebrate it. There is no recorded celebration of the Visitation until Saint Bonaventure, a Franciscan, recommended it in 1263. It was not until 1389 that Pope Urban VI officially inserted it in the liturgical calendar at 2 July. Its theological importance stems from the tradition that, after Mary, Christians regarded the foetal Baptist as the first human being to have perceived the physical presence of the Incarnated Christ as a divine embryo in the womb of Mary. This perception by the Baptist is an interpretation of the words Luke cites Elizabeth as uttering upon meeting Mary: "For indeed, as soon as the voice of your greeting sounded in my ears, the babe leaped in my womb for joy. (*Luke* 1:44)"

Chartres - The Disconnected Zodiac

Thus, the Christian symbolism of these two feast days as representative of the Incarnation has strong and easily understood semantic connections to the Gospel narratives. The Royal Portal sculptures emphasize these connections further because they depict both the Annunciation and the Visitation in the lower lintel over the Incarnation door, along with the Nativity and the Annunciation to the Shepherds. You can see them in Figure 2, position 59. Moreover, the Annunciation, the Visitation and the Baptism of Jesus are all emphasised again above the Royal Portal in the centre lancet window among a set of 24 images that illustrate the key moments in the early life of Jesus. Accordingly, as Fassler proposes, the semantic connections between the Incarnation and the two feast days are abundantly clear.

Pairing of Signs and Months

Fassler's explanation relies on a method of pairing the Signs and Months that was preferred at Chartres. Medieval art very frequently pairs, one to one, the 12 Signs of the Zodiac with the 12 months of the calendar. These pairings are always a bit awkward. The day the Sun enters a given Sign is always around the 20th day of a calendar month. The Sun stays in that Sign for about 30 days and then it enters the next Sign on or about the 20th of the next month. Accordingly, if you want to use a given Sign to symbolize or pair with a given month in a visual image, there is a choice to make. One choice is to pair the month with the Sign the Sun enters in that month – the Entry method. The other choice is to pair the Sign with the following month because during the following month, the Sun stays in that Sign for a longer time – the Duration method. For example, the Sun enters the Sign Pisces on (or about) February 19 and stays in Pisces until about March 20. The Entry method pairs Pisces with February, while the Duration method pairs it with March, as listed in Table 1.

Table 1 – Sign/Month Pairing Methods

Sign	Month	
	Entry	Duration
Aquarius	January	February
Pisces	February	March
Aries	March	April
Taurus	April	May
Gemini	May	June
Cancer	June	July
Leo	July	August
Virgo	August	September
Libra	September	October
Scorpio	October	November
Sagittarius	November	December
Capricorn	December	January

Chartres - The Disconnected Zodiac

The Entry Method

Throughout the medieval period, the vast majority of sculptures, stained glass, manuscript illuminations, calendars, Books of Hours, breviaries, psalters and such, generally use the Entry method when pairing the Signs and Months. The pairings in the Zodiac Window, in Figure 7, follow the Entry method. Another example, in Figure 13 from the *Hunterian Psalter*, a manuscript dated *ca.* 1170, shows pairings of February/Pisces, March/Aries, May/Gemini and June/Cancer, following the Entry method.

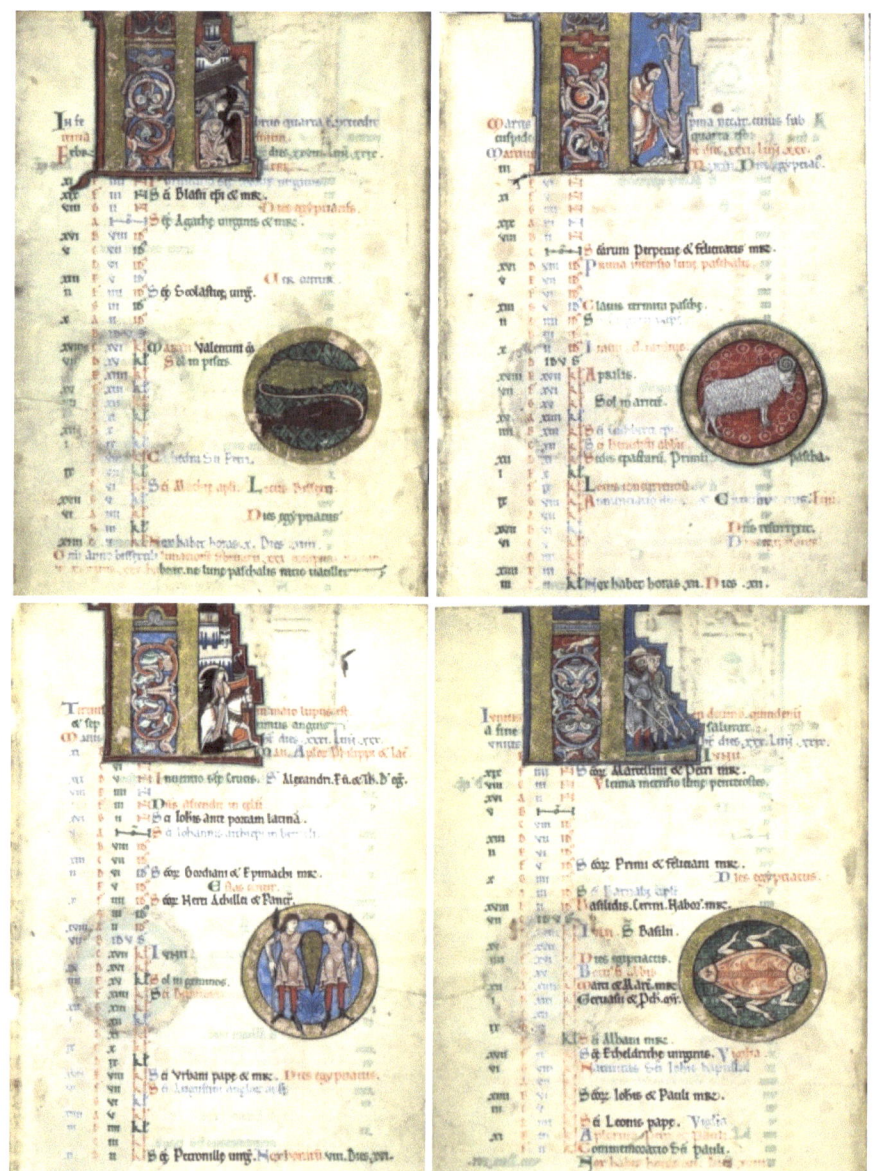

Figure 13 - The Hunterian Psalter (*circa* 1170) with pairings of February/Pisces, March/Aries, May/Gemini and June/Cancer, based on the month in which the Sun enters the Signs.

Images from Glasgow University Library MS Hunter 229 (U.3.2).
https://www.gla.ac.uk/myglasgow/library/files/special/exhibns/psalter/psalterindex.html

Chartres -The Disconnected Zodiac

The use of the Entry method is so predominant in art during all of the middle Ages that even the best historians of art omit mention of the Duration method for the sake of simplicity. For example, in 2007 Colum Hourihane published what is possibly the best currently available inventory of the depiction of the Signs of the Zodiac and the Labours of the Months in medieval art.[16] His book is an unrivalled visual record of these images. At the time, he was the Director of Princeton University's Index of Christian Art, a collection of comprehensive files that fully document images of this kind. If you were to read only his introductory summary description of the Signs, you would think that medieval artists only ever used the Entry method. Hourihane's simplified introductory summary of the Signs does not even acknowledge that the Duration method exists.[17]

To be fair, the body of the book does include examples of both methods. The introduction also says that so many variations exist that, "Even within one sequence it is possible to find many variations from the standard; in compiling this catalogue I came to expect the unexpected, which is one reason why the subject has taken so long to document."[18]

The only art historian I know of who explicitly describes both methods in reference to Chartres is Adolf Katzenellenbogen. Describing the Duration Method used in the archivolts of the Royal Portal, he writes, "There apparently was a predilection at Chartres for this pattern."[19] He also mentions its use at Chartres in the archivolts of the North Transept Porch.

One solution, that altogether sidesteps the one-to-one pairing of Sign to Month, is simply to show both zodiacal signs occupied by the Sun's position in any given month, essentially combining the Entry and Duration methods into a single image. This is the approach later adopted by the Limbourg Brothers, *ca.* 1416, in their illuminated manuscript known today as *Les très riches heures du Duc de Berry*. On its calendar pages it shows two Signs for each Month, as for example, seen in Figure 14 the page for March showing both Pisces and Aries.

Chartres -The Disconnected Zodiac

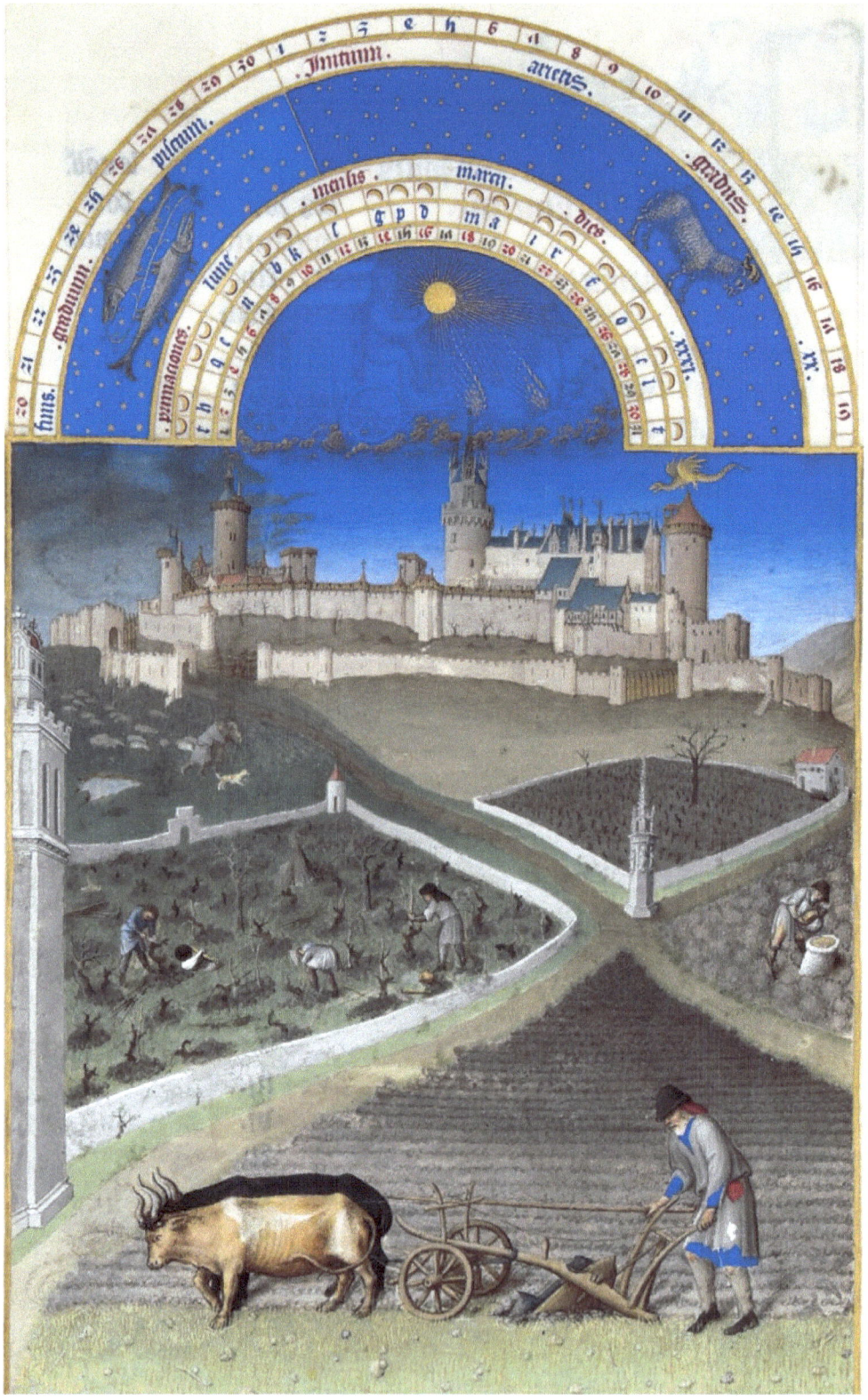

Figure 14 – Month of March with both Pisces and Aries in *Les Très Riches Heures du Duc de Berry*. Image : public domain R.M.N. / R.-G. Ojéda,
https://commons.wikimedia.org/wiki/File:Les_Tr%C3%A8s_Riches_Heures_du_duc_de_Berry_mars.jpg

Chartres - The Disconnected Zodiac

The Duration Method

The Duration method pairs Pisces with March instead of February because the Sun spends more time in Pisces during March than during February. Fassler's explanation recognizes the use of the Duration method in the Royal Portal. Katzenellenbogen also sees it in the North Transept Porch noting it represents a common departure from typical medieval practice and one preferred at Chartres. These observations however are inconsistent with the pairings of the later Zodiac Window, which uses the Entry method, as seen in Figure 24, for example, a close-up of the pane that pairs May with Gemini.

Fassler and Katzenellenbogen both cite the 1893 work of René Merlet and Alexandre Clerval on an exceptionally well-preserved 11th century manuscript from Chartres.[20] The manuscript is a compilation of numerous documents, some dating from as early as 1070. It includes several layers of additions by several medieval hands up to as late as the 1150's. These on-going additions indicate that Chartrians continuously worked with the manuscript over some 180 years, including the years during which they built the Royal Portal, *ca.* 1145. Merlet and Clerval reproduce the miniature illuminations from the manuscript that show pairings of the Months and Signs. As shown in Figure 15, the manuscript uses the Duration method exclusively, pairing Pisces with March and Gemini with June. Accordingly, there can be no question that in the minds of the Chartrian functionaries whose duty it was to work with this manuscript, as Fassler says, Pisces and Gemini, respectively, symbolically represented the months of March and June.

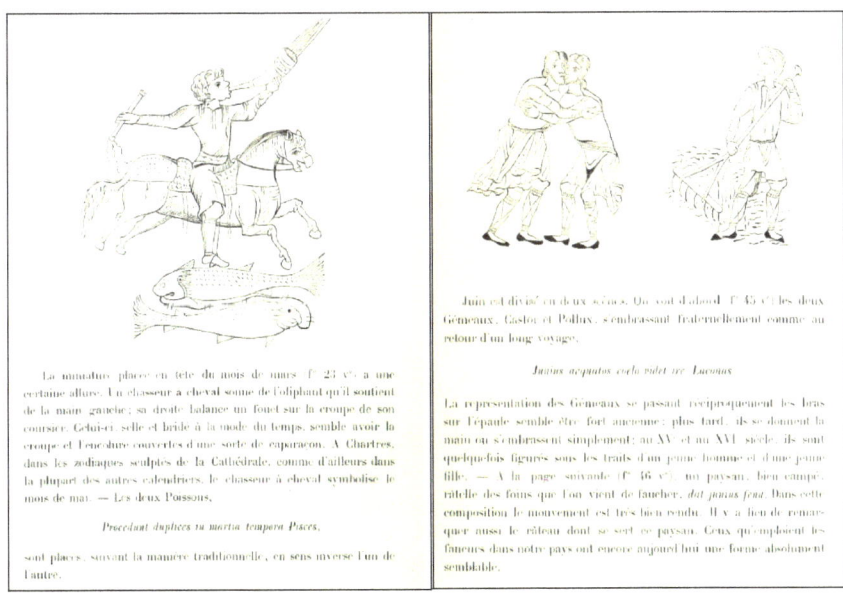

Figure 15- Duration Method Pairing of March with Pisces and of June with Gemini as illustrated and described in *Un manuscrit chartrain du XIe siècle* (A Chartrian Manuscript of the 11th Century) by Merlet and Clerval 1893, pages 12 and 15.
https://archive.org/details/unmanuscritchart00merl/page/n15/mode/2up

Chartres -The Disconnected Zodiac

The Pisces Sculpture

With only one exception, all the sculptures of the Signs over the Royal Portal doors emphasize, in terms of the number, size and placement of elements in the individual sculptures, the Signs themselves. This is clear in the close-ups in Figures 4 and 5. In all cases, it is the Sign itself that is the largest and most dominant image in the sculpture, with the sole exception of Pisces. Here, it is not the traditional two-fish symbol of Pisces that dominates. For some reason, it is the foliage of three trees in which two birds are perched that dominates. Moreover, in the close-up photograph in Figure 4, only one of the two fishes of the traditional Pisces icon is visible, washed ashore at the foot of the trees. While there is no second fish, the iconic string that traditionally binds the two fishes of Pisces is also clearly visible. Traditional star lore has it that this string represents the Arabic name of *Alpha Piscium*, the brightest star in the constellation Pisces. In Arabic the star's name is الرشاء, transliterated as *Alrescha* (alternatively *Al Rescha, Alrischa, Alrisha*), meaning 'the well rope.' It seems odd that the sculpture includes the well rope but not the second fish.

Generally, fish images and the *Ichthys* (ΙΧΘΥC) fish acronym/acrostic have a long and well-established tradition from the second century onward, as being symbolic of Christ.[21,22] Accordingly, I think the three trees and two birds here are an allusion, a symbolic reference to the three crosses as narrated in the Gospels (*Matthew* 27:38, *Mark* 15:27-28,32, *Luke* 23:33, *John* 19:18). The single fish represents Christ and the two birds, the souls of the two thieves. Nevertheless, at the same time, the presence of the Well Rope leaves us in no doubt that the image is also a depiction of Pisces.

It may be that the missing fish of Pisces is a consequence of the trimming of some of the stones after they were sculpted, to fit a smaller space than they were originally expected to fit. The images on numerous stones in the archivolts of the Royal Portal, seen in Figure 1 and in Figure 2, appear to be truncated and incomplete. Pisces is missing a fish. One of the shepherds is definitely cut vertically in half (Figure 2 position 59, right edge). July's cereal harvester is cut off above the knees, as are Aristotle and Pythagoras. October's fruit harvester is cut below the knees. January's two-faced Janus is cut through his feasting table. These trimmings and truncations are evidence that the sculptures were originally made to fit a much larger space that could have accommodated them without trimming. It is possible that they may be spolia, materials and artwork salvaged from another building and repurposed at Chartres. Another more likely explanation is that the trimming was required by a design change that took place after the sculpting was done but before the stones were installed. It may be that an original design called for the façade of the cathedral to be set back, behind and fully

Chartres -The Disconnected Zodiac

detached from the two towers. This would have provided more than double the narrow space between the two towers, as depicted in Figure 16.

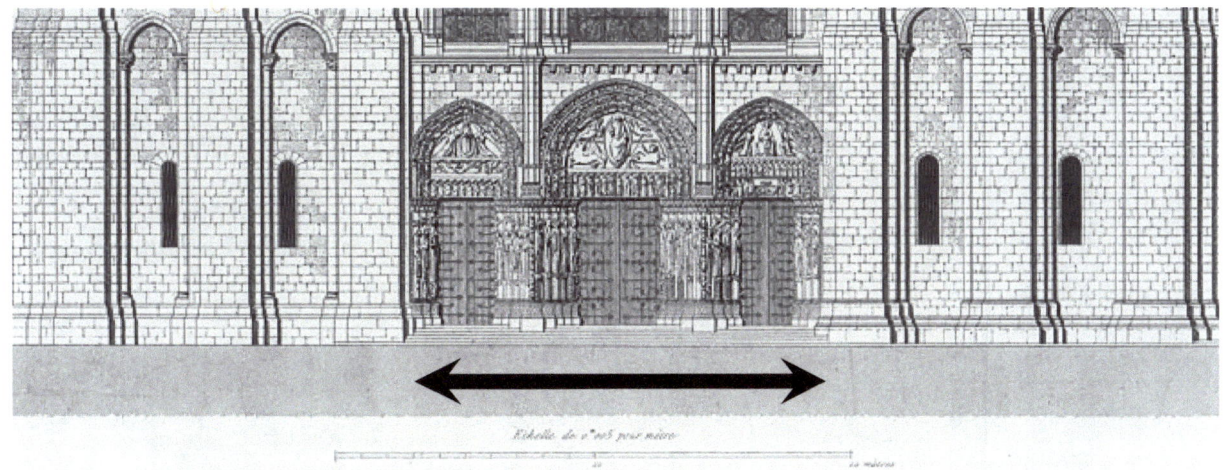

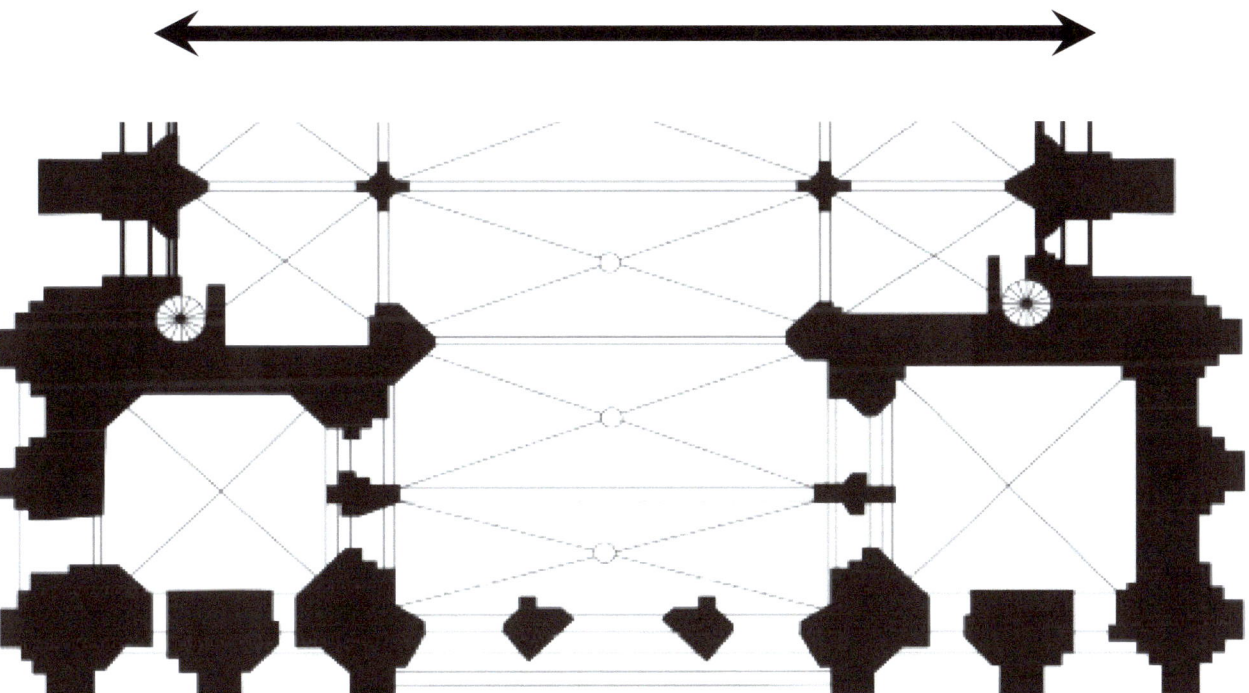

Figure 16 – Elevation and Plan of the Royal Portal Façade. The short black arrow shows the actual width of the Royal Portal between the two towers. The longer black arrow shows the greater width that would have been available on a façade set back behind and detached from the two towers.

Elevation: Adapted from *Monographie de la cathédrale de Chartres,*. Atlas. Planche n°4 : façade occidentale - Gravure., Paris, Imprimerie impériale, 1867. Image cropped from:
https://commons.wikimedia.org/wiki/File:Monografie_de_la_Cathedrale_de_Chartres_-_04_Facade_occidentale_-_Gravure.jpg

Plan: Adapted from *Die Kirchliche Baukunst des Abendlandes*, G. Dehio and G. von Bezold, , Stuttgart, 1887-1902, plate 383 Lithograph. Image cropped from: Gothika,
https://upload.wikimedia.org/wikipedia/commons/thumb/e/e3/Chartres.svg/2560px-Chartres.svg.png

Chartres - The Disconnected Zodiac

The Gemini Sculpture

The Gemini sculpture over the Incarnation door is seen in context in Figure 2 and in close-up in Figure 4. It places the twins behind an inordinately large shield, a detail of which is seen in Figure 17. Medieval depictions of the Gemini Twins placed behind or flanking a shield are common. In the Royal Portal, however, the size of the Gemini Shield seems exceptionally emphasized. The shield is so big it reaches from the toes of the twins, on which its point rests, to the top of their chest. It has an ornate border surrounding what I at first took to be an eight-rayed starburst, the longest ray of which reaches downward to the tapered point of the shield. Curiously, both the tapered point and the Twins' toes on which it rests eye-catchingly protrude beyond the edge of the pedestal.

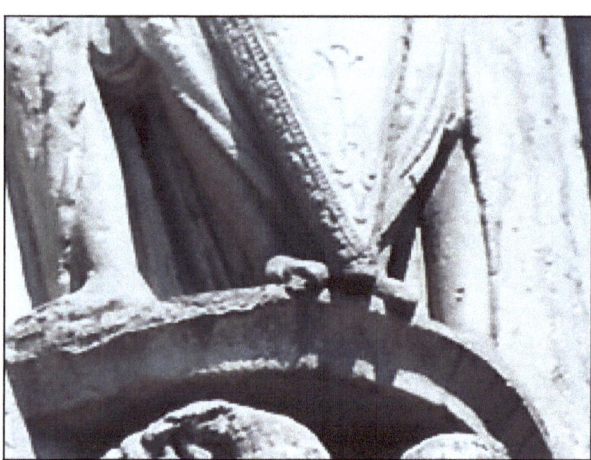

Figure 17 – Detail of Gemini Sculpture with the Twins' toes and the tip of an inordinately large shield protruding beyond the edge of the pedestal. Image: Vanderbilt University, cropped from URL: https://diglib.library.vanderbilt.edu//act-imagelink.pl?RC=26309

Baptism as Shield

From as early as the 1st Century, there is a well-documented Christian tradition of the Shield as a metaphor for Baptism. In a letter to Polycarp, Bishop of Smyrna, Ignatius of Antioch (c. 35 – c. 107) wrote: "Let your baptism abide as your shield, your faith as your helmet, your love as your spear, your patience as your body-armour."[23] The *Epistle of Paul to the Ephesians* provides a precedent for the metaphoric imagery of the Armor of God used by Ignatius:

> Wherefore take unto you the whole *armour of God*, that ye may be able to withstand in the evil day, and having done all, to stand. Stand therefore, having your loins girt about with truth, and having on *the breastplate of righteousness*; and your feet shod with the preparation of the gospel of peace; above all, taking *the shield of faith*, wherewith ye shall be able to quench all the fiery darts of the wicked. And take *the helmet of salvation*, and the sword of the Spirit, which is the word of God. (*Ephesians* 6:13-17 KJV, my emphasis)

The life and letters of Ignatius of Antioch were widely known from the earliest days of Christianity by the likes of Eusebius, Jerome, John Chrysostom and Origen. These days, the letters of Ignatius are under serious challenge as forgeries. However, such

Chartres - The Disconnected Zodiac

challenges have no bearing on the oral and written transmission of their ideas and metaphors from generation to generation, country to country, language to language and medium to medium. If the Baptism-as-Shield metaphor of Ignatius (or his forgers) found its way into 12th Century Chartrian sculpture, as a symbol of the Baptist, then this is additional evidence that corroborates Fassler's view.

Heraldic Insignia of Navarre and Blois

On closer inspection, the starburst on the shield is strikingly similar to, if not identical with, the carbuncles or chains in the arms and heraldic insignia of the 10th, 11th and 12th century House of Navarre: *de gueules, aux rais d'escarboucle d'or* (of red with golden carbuncles radiant) and later *"de gueules aux chaînes d'or posées en orle, en croix et en sautoir, chargées en cœur d'une émeraude au naturel"* (of red with golden chains in orle, cross and saltire, charged in the heart with a natural emerald). The quite different Arms of Blois - *d'azur à une bande d'argent* (of blue banded in silver) appear in the bottom pane of the Zodiac window on the shield of Thibaut VI (died 1218), count of Blois and Clermont-en-Beauvaisis, seen in Figure 7, position 2. Figure 18 and Figure 19 show more images of these heraldic devices.

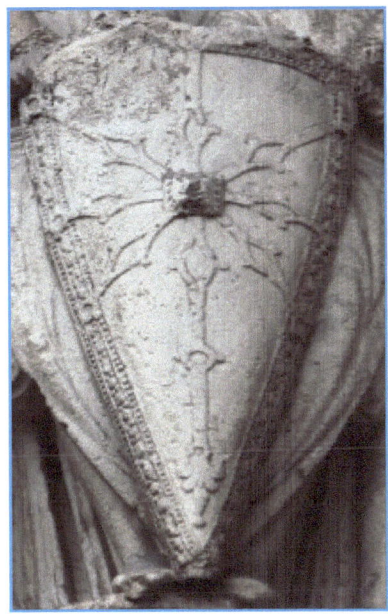 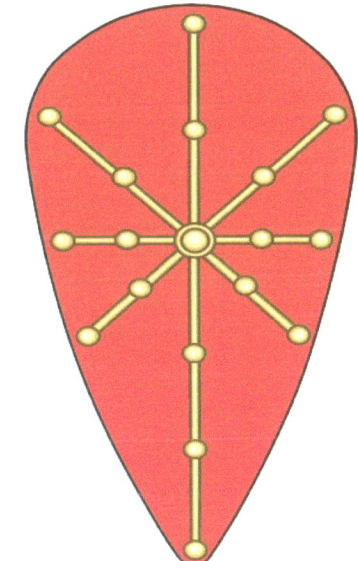 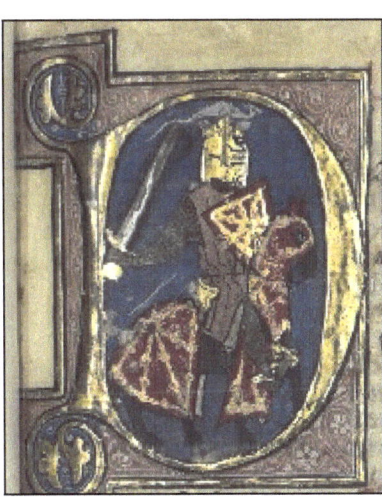

Figure 18 – Shield of Gemini and Heraldic Insignia of Navarre

Left: The Royal Portal Shield of Gemini

Center: Arms of Sancho VI, King of Navarre called the Wise, from 1150 until 1194. Arms: *"de gueules, aux rais d'escarboucle d'or."*

Right: Thibaut I de Navarre *chevauchant* **with Arms of Navarre** *"de gueules aux chaînes d'or posées en orle, en croix et en sautoir, chargées en cœur d'une émeraude au naturel."*
http://visualiseur.bnf.fr/Visualiseur?Destination=Mandragore&O=06000794&E=13&I=99610&M=imageseule
https://commons.wikimedia.org/wiki/File:Theobald_I_of_Navarre_2.jpg

Chartres - The Disconnected Zodiac

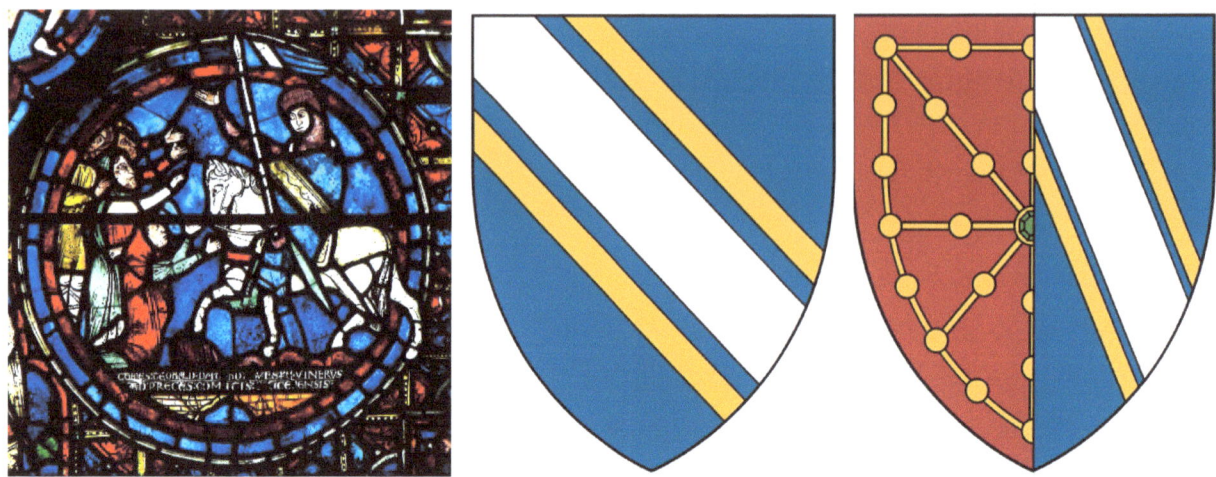

Figure 19– Arms of Blois and Navarre

Left: Chartres Zodiac Window Detail - Thibaut VI (1190-1218) count of Chartres, donor on behalf of Thomas count of Perche, and Vintners. Image https://fr.wikipedia.org/wiki/Thibaut_VI_de_Blois

Center: Arms of the House of Blois-Champagne http://wappenwiki.org/index.php?title=House_of_Blois-Champagne

Right: Arms of the Kingdom of Navarre, House of Blois 1234-1284
http://wappenwiki.org/index.php?title=Kingdom_of_Navarre

A later Blois, Thibaut IV (1201-1253), count of Champagne, inherited the Kingdom of Navarre through his mother Blanche of Navarre, the sister of Sancho VI of Navarre, becoming the first French ruler of Navarre in 1234, as Thibaut I of Navarre. Considering the military, political and governance roles played in this region and at this time by members of the Houses of Navarre and of Blois with intermarriage between them, the shields, emblazoned with their arms must carry the additional symbolic load of representing these families.

The Wisdom of the Navarrese Gemini/Jiménez

The word Gemini is an obvious pun on the Spanish surname *Jiménez*. García Jiménez I, was King of Navarre and Aragon in the late 9th century and founder of the House of Jiménez, one of the ruling families of Navarre. He was the first to adopt the Arms of Navarre seen in Figure 18. His descendant Sancho Garcés VI was called *Sancho the Wise*, a sobriquet that, in the context of Christian monarchs, alludes to the wise rulership of the Biblical Solomon and a keen interest in higher learning. After only three more generations, the same sobriquet would be given to a direct Jiménez descendant, Alphonse X of Castile, sponsor of the famous *Alphonsine Tables*, instrumental to Copernicus and the scientific revolution his astronomy triggered.

Chartres - The Disconnected Zodiac

I think the fact that the Arms of Navarre and of Blois turn up at Chartres in the company of these glass and stone Zodiac images, communicates an exceptional interest within these families at the time in higher learning in general and Astronomy in particular. This was an interest evidently shared with the Masters of the School of Chartres, and an indication of how very well connected these Chartrians were.

Selection of Pisces and Gemini

It is evident that some of the sculptural artwork above the doors of the Royal Portal was trimmed to fit a tighter space. Regardless of whether this was because of ill-fitting spolia, an inconvenient design change or any other reason, it remains a fact that somebody at some point made a decision to select Pisces and Gemini, rather than any of the other 10 signs or 12 months to be set apart and placed together over the Right Door. This decision cannot have been made without some deliberation and consideration of the meaning that the selection would convey. It is also important to note that whoever made this decision, also considered it appropriate to sacrifice the second fish of Pisces, while preserving the full length of Gemini. Any explanation of the full meaning conveyed by the Disconnected Zodiac must answer, first, why Pisces and Gemini were selected over the other signs and months, and secondly, why the full length of Gemini was given priority over the missing fish of Pisces.

There is additional significance in the Gemini Shield in that its placement, size, extended bottom carbuncle and tapered shape have the visual effect of drawing the eye downwards toward the feet of Gemini with their overhanging toes pointing to the Pisces image beneath it. Though there is more to say about the feet of Gemini, at this stage I want to stress three points arising from the historical details and cultural context of Fassler's view.

Fassler's View Assessed

First, the Baptism-as-Shield metaphor of Ignatius, though Fassler does not mention it, is additional evidence as a precedent that reinforces her idea that the Royal Portal Sign of Gemini with its inordinately large shield does indeed have a historically verifiable symbolic and semantic connection to the Baptist and baptism. Coupled with Pisces as a symbol of Christ, the two images are loaded with semantic connections to the full baggage of the Christian theology of the Fall, of the Incarnation and of Redemption. After reviewing the evidence, I think Fassler's interpretation makes perfect sense because of its sound analogical reasoning against the right evidence from the right place and from the right time. Her religious interpretation is unimpeachable. At the same time, it is also a bit incomplete because it only scratches the surface by addressing but one of several layers of meaning. Her interpretation succeeds in extracting true meaning from the symbols, but not all of it.

Second, the heraldic symbolism on the shield demonstrates that these images often reach beyond religious symbolism as multi-valent carriers of multiple meaning. In this case, the symbolic connections are to important dynastic, political and military significance and they need to be considered in addition to Fassler's religious interpretation.

Third, therefore, it is important to ask whether there is yet more evidence to consider and to explore additional levels of meaning beyond these religious and political connections. In spite of all the evidence considered so far, a certain sense of dissatisfaction remains because Fassler's religious interpretation, and my own political one, leave several important questions unanswered and other lines of evidence unexplored. There are many liturgical calendar dates other than the June feast of the Baptist that could have been used equally well or with even greater significance in connection with the idea of the Incarnation. These include Advent between 27 November and 3 December in Sagittarius, the Nativity itself on December 25 in Capricorn, Epiphany on 6 January in Capricorn, the Presentation of Jesus at the Temple (Candlemas) on 2 February in Aquarius, or the Transfiguration of Jesus on 6 August in Leo. Among these other dates, it seems to me that the Nativity itself ought to have outranked the Baptist's feast day. Is Jesus himself not more relevant to the Incarnation than the Baptist? Moreover, if the objective was to convey no more than the idea of March and June, why bother using Zodiac Signs at all? Would it not make more sense to have used images of the months themselves – tree pruning in March and planting in June? A more complete explanation of the two disconnected Signs needs to address these questions. To do that I think it is important to look beyond the microcosmic day-to-day symbolism of the liturgical calendar, and the mundane political history. Accordingly, by turning my attention upward toward loftier ideas of medieval Theology, Natural Philosophy and Astronomy, I think it is possible to provide a more complete understanding of how the Zodiac anomalies convey deeper meaning connected to the larger macrocosmic concept of the entire Christian cosmos including the full sweep of Biblical time.

Chartres - The Disconnected Zodiac

5. MORE CONTEXT AND A NEW HYPOTHESIS

Wisdom and Science in the Symbols

As seen in Figure 2 and mapped in Figure 6, the two disconnected Signs are located among a double set of images that are symbolic of wisdom and the teaching syllabus of the *trivium* and *quadrivium* of late pagan antiquity. The archivolt images surround the Virgin and Christ Child in a traditional *sedes sapientiae* (Latin for: throne of wisdom) pose. Accordingly, I think it makes sense to look for additional meaning in readings and texts of Theology and Natural Philosophy, subjects for which the Masters of the School of Chartres were then, and are to this day, most well-known. Some of the readings available to the Chartrian community *circa* 1145 are listed in Table 2.

The anomalous Zodiac sculptures fit with the overall theme of the entire Royal Portal as a depiction of the theological concept of time using the three key moments of time in Christian theology: Creation, Incarnation and Second Coming. Placed in the context of the *quadrivium*, teachings that deal with numbers, order, quantity and measurement, it makes sense that the two disconnected Signs would have something to do with using astronomical science to measure and quantify time. The additional depiction over the centre door of astrolabes, shown in Figure 20, is consistent with this idea because astrolabes are scientific instruments of astronomical measurement and computation associated primarily with orderly and quantified observation, sky mapping and timekeeping.

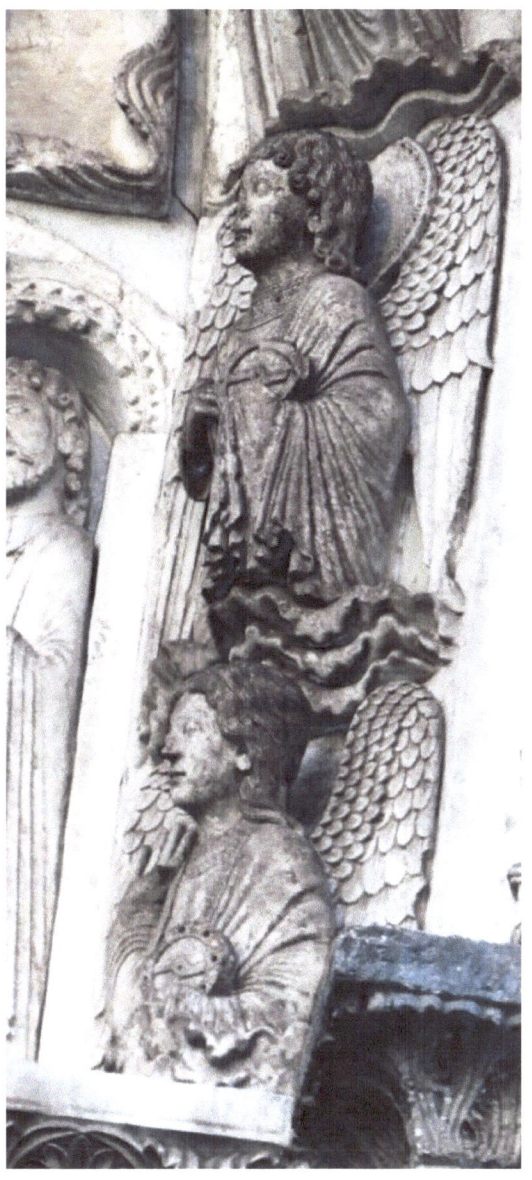

Figure 20 – Angels Unwrapping Astrolabes in the archivolts of the Royal Portal, centre door *ca.* 1145. Image: Legault

Chartres -The Disconnected Zodiac

Table 2– Readings Available at Chartres *circa* **1145 AD** (adapted from Knitter 2000, page 62: https://scholarworks.sjsu.edu/etd_theses/2052).

Library of St. Peter's Monastary		Other Libraries
Religious (70 Volumes)	**Secular (20 Volumes)**	
Old & New Testaments	Albinus, Geometry	Boethius
Psalters	Antidotaria, Medical Prescriptions	Cicero
Commentaries thereon	Aphorismi, Yppocratis	Livy
Conciliar Canons	Bede, History	Pliny
Capitularies	Boethius, Music and Arithmetic	Quintilian on Rhetoric
Lives of Saints	Concordia, Yppocratis	
Amalarius	Donatius, Grammar	
Ambrose	Gregory of Tours, History	
Augustine	Josephus, History	
Bacharius	Podismus, Nipsius	
Cyprian	Priscian, Grammar	
Cassiodorus	Prophyry, "Isagoge"	
Pseudo-Dionysus	Fortunatus	
Flugentius	Juvenal	
Gregory the Great	Marcianus Capella	
Gregory of Tours	Ovid	
Isidore of Seville	Virgil	
Jerome	Cicero	
Origen		
Rabanus		
Mavrus		
Others less eminent		

Hypothesis

I think the deliberate selection of Pisces and Gemini for separate placement over the Incarnation door is a visual metaphor that symbolically represents a bracketing of the amount of time from Creation to the Incarnation. The Chartrian Masters knew the numerical methods of the *quadrivium*, including astronomy and the concept of astronomical precession. The two disconnected Signs may represent an early application of what we now call Zodiacal Ages to represent the estimated duration of the Old Testament period as spanning from early in the Age of Gemini to the beginning of the Age of Pisces. I will now review historical evidence to explain this hypothesis.

Chartres -The Disconnected Zodiac

Year of Creation

It is well known that Christians from the earliest times were intensely preoccupied over how old Creation was. For instance, Theophilus of Antioch counting from the year 169 concluded: "All the years from the creation of the world amount to a total of 5698 years, and the odd months and days."[24] Restating his estimate from the birth of Christ in year 1 gives the year of Creation as 5529 BC. Many estimates of this kind were widely known in medieval times from numerous writers and traditions that had used biblical chronologies and other methods to calculate the year of Creation. Table 3 lists over a dozen of these estimates. The average of this list puts the biblical count from Creation to Incarnation at 5,342 years with a standard deviation of about 400 years or 7 percent of the average. This is a reasonably good match with the traditional *Anno Mundi* (Year of the World) count of 5,500 BC. Texts of many of these authors and of others who cited them were available for reading in Chartres at the time of Thierry of Chartres' Chancellorship.

Table 3 – Year of Creation: Estimates by Christian authors from late Roman times to the early medieval period.

Author	Approximate Date (AD)		Estimated Year of Creation (BC)
	Birth	Death	
Theophilus of Antioch		181	5529
Clement of Alexandria	150	215	5592
Sextus Julius Africanus	160	240	5501
Hippolytus of Rome	170	235	5500
Eusebius of Caesarea	260	339	5228
Panodorus of Alexandria	-	400	5493
Traditional Byzantine date	400	-	5509
Jerome	347	420	5199
Sulpicius Severus	363	425	5469
Gregory of Tours	538	594	5500
Isidore of Seville	560	636	5336
Maximus the Confessor	580	662	5493
Bede	673	735	3952
George Syncellus	-	810	5492
		Average	5342

Bi-directional Reading

Bi-directional reading is required to understand the elaborately unconventional chronological order of the Signs and Months sculptures of the Royal Portal. There, the four seasons are each represented by a grouping of three pairs of Months and Signs. The positioning of the pairs is not side by side but with the Sign above the Month. The flow of time in each season group begins at the bottom of the archivolt and runs upward to end at the top-middle. Thus, the flow of time runs in two directions: clockwise on the left and counter-clockwise on the right. Figure 3 provides a table and a sketch of this highly unusual arrangement. Two of the twelve pairs are incomplete because Pisces and Gemini are missing. Nevertheless, it is evident from the ten pairings displayed that the sculptures use the Duration method applied in a bi-directional manner. As we saw from the findings of Fassler, Katzenellenbogen and Merlet, the

Chartres -The Disconnected Zodiac

Duration method was preferred at Chartres at the time. As noted at the bottom of the sketch in Figure 3 the chronological order of seasons is presented reading from right to left, yet another reversal of direction from the more usual convention of showing the flow of time going from left to right.

Measuring Time

In the context of imagery involving both the Zodiac and the medieval educational curriculum, there is really only one situation that calls for bi-directional readings and reversals of direction. This arises in the medieval astronomical techniques used to measure time. To measure the hours of the day you follow the Sun in one direction east to west from sunrise to sunset. To measure the year, you change directions to follow the Sun through the Zodiac from west to east. To measure much longer periods, you change directions again to follow the movement of the two equinoctial points from east to west: the precession of the equinoxes. Reasoning by analogy with the idea of bi-directional reading of celestial motions in medieval astronomy, provides a clue or a key to understanding the meaning of the Zodiac anomalies.

Medieval Astronomy at Chartres

The known contents of Thierry of Chartres' book *Heptateuchon*, listed in Table 4, provides good evidence that knowledge of the astronomy of Ptolemy, Hyginus, and Al-Kwarizmi was at hand among the Chartrians.[25] This knowledge included the concept of astronomical precession, understood as the very slow movement of the position of the equinoxes through the constellations of the Zodiac.

Modern Precession

What modern astronomy now calls *general precession* is the observation that the positions of the equinoxes – the two points where the celestial equator intersects the ecliptic - slowly move relative to the background stars. Equinox events occur twice annually when the Sun's position moves onto one of these two intersection points. Their movement takes place at a rate very close to 50.29 arc seconds retrograde per year. This is equal to one full degree of arc in just over 71.5 years or one full 30-degree Sign of the Zodiac in about 2,145 years. Professor Roy Bishop provides an excellent and up to date description of precession in the *Observer's Handbook 2017* of the Royal Astronomical Society of Canada:

> As a result of the combined precession of the equator and precession of the ecliptic, the equinoxes (the intersection points of the celestial equator and the ecliptic) drift westward (retrograde) about 50.29″ per year (a period of

Chartres - The Disconnected Zodiac

approximately 25,800 years. [...] The Vernal equinox was located in the constellation Gemini 7,500 years ago [*ca.* 5483 BC], in Taurus 4500 years ago, and in Aries 3000 years ago. It moved into Pisces from the "first point of Aries" around the beginning of the Christian era 2000 years ago, at roughly the same time as Hipparchus discovered the precession of the equinoxes.[26]

Table 4 - Contents of Thierry of Chartres' *Heptateuchon* (Knitter 2000)	
Contents of the *Heptateuchon* taken from MS. 497 and MS. 498	Boethius *Introductio ad syllogismos categoricos*
	Boethius *De syllogismo categorico*
MS. 497	Apuleius *Perihermenias*
Prologue	Boethius *De syllogismis hypotheticis*
A. Grammar	Cicero *Topics*
Accessus to Donatus	Boethius *De Differentiis topicis*
Donatus *Ars Minor*	Boethius *de divisione*
Prima declinatio quot litteras terminales...futuri ut audiendus (An elementary dialogue continuing the *Ars Minor*)	Marius Victorinus *De definitione* (attributed to Boethius here)
Preface to Donatus *Ars Major*	**D. Arithmetic**
Donatus *Ars Major*	Boethius *Arithmetica*
Priscian *Institutiones Grammaticae*	Gebert of Aurillac *Scholium in Arithmetica*
Priscian's own preface to the series of minor works of Priscian	Martianus Capella *De Nuptiis Mercurii et Philologe*, Book VII
Priscian *De figuris numerorum*	Euclid *Elements*, Books VII-IX, Adelard of Bath's Aribic translation
Priscian *De metris fabularum Terentii*	**E. Music**
Priscian *De accentibus*	Boethius *Musica*
Preface to Priscian *De duodecim versibus Virgilii*	**F. Geometry**
Priscian *De duodecim versibus Virgilii*	Euclid *Elements*, Books XIV, prop. 7-XV, Adelard of Bath's Aribic translat
Priscian *De nomine, pronomine et verbo*	'Boethius' *Geometria I*, Book V, chapters 1, 6, 7, 8 (Thierry corrected Boethius' text)
Que est agnitio prime declinationis pronominis?... vestras vestratis; cuias, cuiatis.	Excerps from Nipsus, Epaphroditus and Vitruvius Rufus: *Mensurarum tria genera ... erit diamentrum circuli*
Donatus *Ars grammatica*	*Mensura est quicquid pondere* (the opening to Isidore *Etymologiae* XV and 'Boethius' *Geometria V*, sec. A.
De posituris	Fragment on hexagon and octagon
B. Rhetoric	Columella *De re rustica*
Cicero *De inventione*	Gromatici and more Balbus
Rhetorica ad Herennium	Fragment of Boethius's translation of Euclid (Book I, definitions)
Cicero *De partitione oratoria*	Gerbert of Aurillac *Geometria*
Julius Severianus *Ars rhetorica*	'Botehius' *Geometria II*
Martianus Capella *De nuptiis*, book V	(The Abacus)
C. Dialectic	Diagram of an abacus
Prophyry *Isagage*, Boethius' translation	*Omnis numerus aut ex digito*
Aristotle *Categoriae*, Boethius' translation	*Si igitur vis scire ... et sint huiusmodi*
Aristotle *De interpretatione*, Boethius' translation	The fraction table of Hermannus Contractus
Aristotle *Prior Analytics*, Boethius' translation	Another table
Aristotle *Topics*, Boethius' translation	Blank pages
MS. 498	**G. Astronomy**
In hoc volumine continentur: liber elencorum Aristotelis logica rethorica arismetia musica mathematica Iulii firmici materni minori, Geometria canones tabule et alia de astronomia	Hyginus *Astronomicon: Studio grammatice artis ... Qui cum sevisset*
	Ptolemy *Canons*
	Astronomical Tables of Ptolemy
Aristotle *Sophistici elenchi*	Al-Khwarizmi, *Tables*, translated by Adelard of Bath

Generally, the rate of precession is measurable by observation of long-term displacement of the Sun's position in the Zodiac on the day of the equinoxes. Considering that precession involves a displacement of the Sun's equinoctial position, and considering that the medieval Sun following Plato's definition was thought of as a planet, precession may be taken as a legitimate platonic 'keeper' or marker to measure the passage of time. Accordingly, NASA's *Dictionary of Technical Terms for Aerospace Use (NASA SP 7, 1965)* says the period of a Great Year or Platonic Year is "one complete cycle of the equinoxes around the ecliptic [i.e. 360 degrees around the Zodiac] is about 25,800 years."[27] Today, a Zodiacal Age is the name used for the amount of time the

Chartres - The Disconnected Zodiac

vernal equinox spends in a given segment of the Zodiac spanning 30 degrees of the Ecliptic or about one twelfth of a Platonic Year (360/30 = 12). Generally omitted in popular descriptions of astronomical precession is the fact that the rate of precession varies slightly over time. Accordingly, astronomers never assign a precise fixed value to the duration of a zodiacal age or a Platonic year; the values they give are always qualified as approximations.

The duration of time you assign to a Zodiacal Age or to a Platonic Year depends directly on the rate of precession you use to calculate it. The inaccurate and excessively slow rate first found by Hipparchus and used by Ptolemy was challenged in the middle ages by Arabic astronomers.

Medieval Precession

The concept of astronomical precession was nothing new to medieval Christianity. In the third century, Origen, some of whose writings were available at Chartres, considered it so well known that he used it to argue that astrological divination and prognostication were fakery and heretical:

> There is a well-known theorem which proves that the Zodiac, like the planets, moves from west to east at the rate of one part in a hundred years, and that this movement in the lapse of so long a time changes the local relation of the signs [...]. We are thus taught that the most learned in these matters cannot show beforehand what the Lord intends to bring upon every nation.   Origen *The Philocalia XXIII, 18* [28]

Origen was not an astronomer and he neglects to mention that the 'one part in a hundred years', is one part out of 360 parts, or one degree of a 360 degree circle. In antiquity, Claudius Ptolemy, following Hipparchus, had put the rate of precession substantially slower than the modern value, at about 1 degree per 100 years, or one full 30-degree Sign of the Zodiac in 3,000 years. This was the rate known to Origen. Later, in medieval times, the Arab astronomer Al-Battani (*ca.* 855 – 929) found Ptolemy failed to agree with observations. Al-Battani had measured the rate of precession as being much faster, a value close to 54.5 arc seconds per year, which is one degree in about 66.1 years or one full 30-degree Sign of the Zodiac every 1,982 years. This is much closer to the modern value of about 2,145 years. Al-Battani wrote about this in his book *Kitab al-Zij*. This book appeared in the Latin West in 1116, translated as *De motu stellarum* (On the Motion of the Stars) by Plato of Tivoli who reportedly worked in Barcelona from 1116 to 1138. [29, 30]

Al-Battani at Chartres

Thierry of Chartres was Chancellor at Chartres during the construction of the Royal Portal. There is solid textual evidence that Thierry and his student, Hermann of

Chartres - The Disconnected Zodiac

Carinthia were familiar with the more advanced astronomy of Al-Battani. The evidence appears in Hermann's Preface to his translation from the Arabic of *The Planisphere* of Claudius Ptolemy. In this Preface, Hermann dedicates his work to his former teacher – Thierry of Chartres - whom he praises as the greatest living master of the liberal arts and of natural philosophy in these words:

> *Quod igitur omnium humanitatis studiorum summa radix et principium est, cui potius destinarem quam tibi, quem primam summamque hoc tempore philosophie sedem atque immobiliter fixam varia tempestate fluitantium studiorum anchoram plane quidem, ut novi, et fateor (nec enim diis placeat me, sicut iners volgus solet, invidia teneat, ut sponte quidem aut mendacio locum prestem aut veritatem dissimulem) tibi, inquam, diligentissime preceptor Theodorice que haut equidem ambigam, Platonis animam celitus iterum mortalibus acomodatam.*   Hermann of Carinthia 1143

(To whom, therefore, can I dedicate that which is the deepest principle and root of all studies of humanity rather than to you, who, I know, and therefore plainly confess, hold the first position in philosophy in these times, and are, as it were, an-unmoveably secure anchor in the turbulent storms of ever-changing doctrines? If it pleases the Gods, may envy not make me, like the indolent masses, voluntarily allow myself to lie, or hide the truth before *you, most worthy teacher Thierry*, in whom, I am convinced, the soul of Plato has once again been brought down from heaven and fitted to mortal man.)   Translation Burnett 1978, my emphasis [31]

The fact that Hermann and Thierry shared knowledge of Al-Battani's work in astronomy is also evident in the Preface in a passage naming Arabic authors and texts of astronomical science, indicating both of them knew these authors and texts very well:

> *Ex quibus et duo Ionica lingua collegit volumina, in primam) Sintasim, in sccundam) [sic] Tetrastim-Arabice dicta Almagesti et Alarba, quorum Almagesti quidem (Hei. p. clxxxv) Albeteni commodissime restringit, Tetrastim vero Albumasar non minus commode exampliat[...]*   Hermann of Carinthia 1143

(From these, and in the Greek tongue, he collected two volumes: the Sintasis for the first discipline, and the Tettastis for the second - in Arabic called the Almagest and the Alarba. '*Al-Battani has appropriately made the Almagest more concise* (?), and Abü Marshar has, no less appropriately, expanded on the Alarba.)

Translation Burnett 1978, my emphasis [32]

The reputation of Al-Battani's work, from its first arrival in Europe to this day, rests mainly on its challenges to Ptolemy's observational accuracy and especially for improving Ptolemy on the rate of precession. No modern biographer fails to mention it.

Dating Creation Using Precession

Anyone using Al-Battani's rate of precession, Biblical traditions dating the time of creation and working backwards from the birth of Christ pegged at year AD 1, the dawn of the Age of Pisces, would situate the Alpha moment of Biblical time – the time of creation - early in the Age of Gemini. Accordingly, the interval of time between Creation and the Incarnation may have been represented over the right door of the Royal Portal using the two Signs Gemini and Pisces as symbolically quantifying a Biblically estimated interval of time between the Age of Gemini and the Age of Pisces, as calculated at Al-Battani's rate in Table **5**.

Chartres -The Disconnected Zodiac

Table 5- Zodiacal Age Duration Using Different Rates of Precession

	Al-Battani 54.5 arc sec. per year.		Hipparchus/Ptolemy 36.0 arc sec. per year.		Modern 50.29 arc sec. per year.	
Age	From	To	From	To	From	To
Pisces	1 AD	1982 AD	1 AD	3001 AD	1 AD	2145 AD
Aries	1983 BC	1 BC	3000 BC	1 BC	2145 BC	1 BC
Taurus	3965 BC	1984 BC	6000 BC	3001 BC	4290 BC	2146 BC
Gemini	5947 BC	3966 BC	9000 BC	6001 BC	6435 BC	4290 BC
An estimated year of creation of 5342 BC would have occurred:	Early during the age of Gemini.		During the age of Taurus.		During the age of Gemini.	

My explanation of the reason for the disconnected placement of Gemini and Pisces over the right door is, of course, a hypothesis. It follows on the facts of cultural context that the Chartrian community and Royal Portal designers, had access to the absolute most recent Latin translations of Arabic and Greek works of astronomy. As Peter Ellard says, "They were on the cutting edge of the natural sciences of their day, and this included the use of astrology [and astronomy] texts from Islamic sources which were only very recently made available."[33] Moreover, this hypothesis is also consistent with the Chartrian interest in, and Royal Portal depictions of the most advanced astronomical technology, the astrolabe, which also had just recently arrived from the Andalusian Arabs. The Chartrians had no hesitation in showing how keen they were about these new teachings by boldly and redundantly depicting no less than six and possibly seven instances[34] of this cutting edge technology over the centre door of their Royal Portal. Accordingly, I think it makes sense to think they were just as keen and had no hesitation of also including imagery depicting the latest and most up to date Arabic teaching from Al Battani about precession.

Armillary Sphere and Astrolabe Technology

Evidence of medieval familiarity with armillary sphere technology appears in the early twelfth century book of Bernardus Silvestris entitled *Experimentarius*. An armillary sphere is depicted in mid-13th century illuminated copy in the Bodleian Library, as shown in Figure 21. Moreover, Peter Dronke reports that Bernardus dedicated another one of his books, the *Cosmographia*, to Thierry of Chartres.[35] Both works are in full keeping with the Chartrian School's keen interest in Platonic Natural Philosophy in general, in Astronomy and Cosmology in particular and in their related technologies.

Gerbert of Aurillac (ca. 946–1003) is reputed to have reintroduced technological knowledge of the astrolabe and armillary sphere from the Andalusian Arabs to Latin

Chartres -The Disconnected Zodiac

West. In time they became the educational tools of choice in the middle Ages for teaching the concepts of celestial motion including precession. The armillary sphere was a mechanical object made of metal rings arranged in a spherical framework representing the outermost of the celestial spheres – the firmament on which the fixed stars were embedded. The dominant feature was two main rings set at an angle of 23.5 degrees to each other, representing the angle made by the ecliptic intersecting the celestial equator.

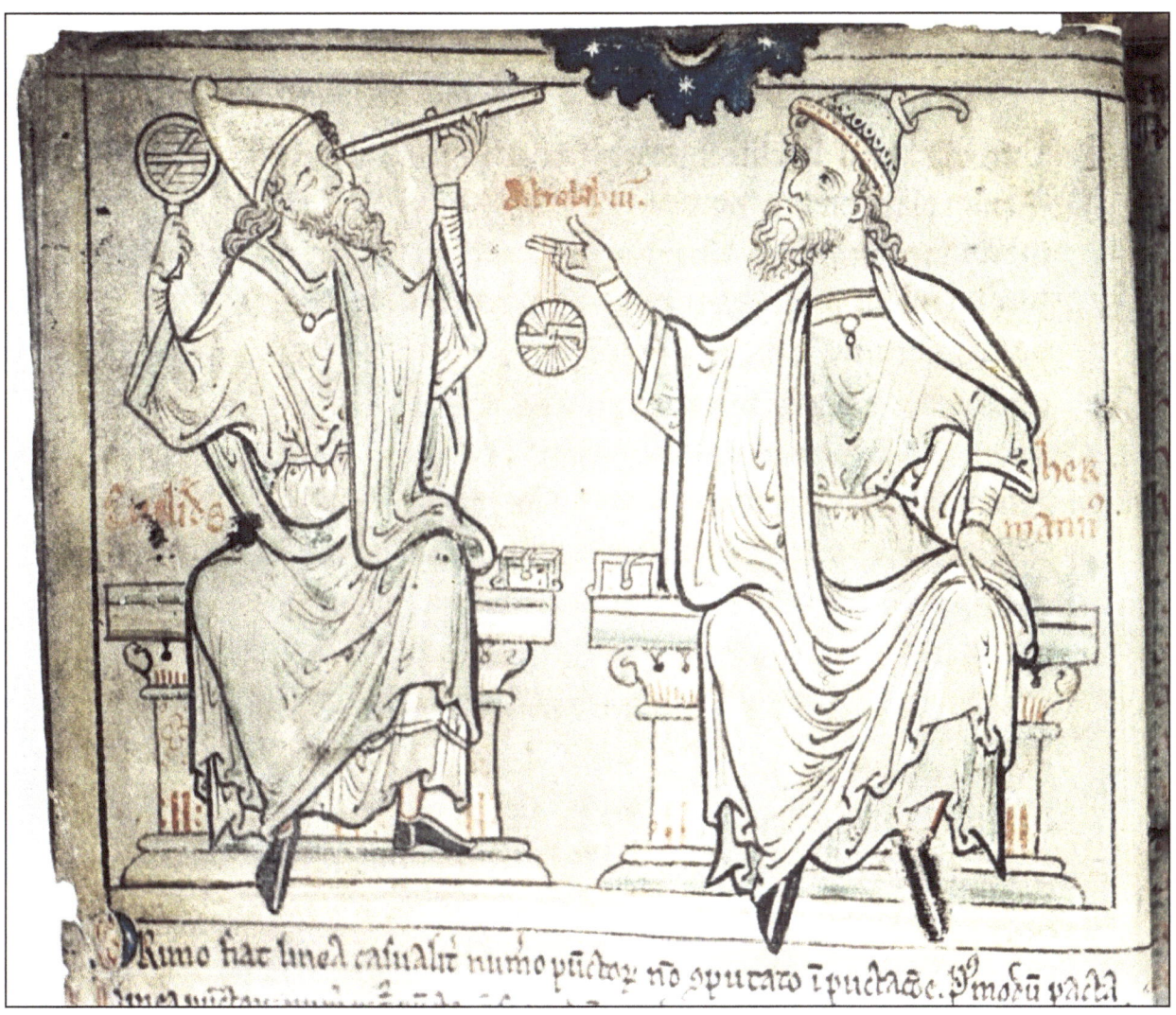

Figure 21 – Armillary Sphere and Astrolabe - Euclid holding armillary sphere and dioptra observing moon and stars, Hermannus holding astrolabe, Bernardus Silverstris *Experimentarius* early 12th century, MS. Ashmole 304 fol. 002v, St. Albans mid-13th century. Image: © Bodleian Libraries, University of Oxford: https://digital.bodleian.ox.ac.uk/inquire/p/7aaf3399-d43e-445f-8705-14f496b2ee80

The ecliptic ring was in fact a metal band of sufficient width to represent the Zodiac wrapped around the celestial sphere. This band was the *armilla* that gives the armillary sphere its name. *Armilla* is the Latin word for an armband. In Roman antiquity, precious

Chartres - The Disconnected Zodiac

metal amrillae could be earned and worn with pride by soldiers as a mark of distinction awarded in recognition of service in armed combat.[36] In the 4th century Latin of the *Vulgate*, an *armilla* was the armband that, along with the crown, was the battlefield regalia of King Saul, removed from his corpse and brought to David:

> So I stood upon him, and slew him, because I was sure that he could not live after that he was fallen: and I took the crown that was upon his head, and the bracelet that was on his arm, and have brought them hither unto my lord.
>
> *II Samuel 1:10, KJV*

On an armillary sphere, and centred on the middle of the armilla, the ecliptic circle was inscribed lengthwise representing the annual path of the Sun through the middle of the Zodiac. The armilla was also divided into 12 equal 30 degree segments. Each segment was inscribed with one of the twelve Signs of the Zodiac. The two intersection points of the armilla and the equatorial ring represented the two equinoctial points. Using an armillary sphere, a teacher could demonstrate to a student how the equinoctial points moved and thus convey an understanding of precession. Medieval armillary spheres included additional rings, visible in Figure 21, appropriately placed parallel to the equatorial ring to represent the tropics of Cancer and Capricorn as well as the Arctic and Antarctic circles. A teacher could use these rings, all tilted at a 23.5 degree angle to the ecliptic ring, to help convey a better understanding of the seasonal movements of the Sun.

As the story goes, teachers had their students imagine a camel crushing an armillary sphere under its foot. The imaginary result would be a more portable flattened sphere or 'planisphere' retaining all of the same information. Thus, the flattened armillary sphere became the astrolabe. Claudius Ptolemy's *Planisphaerium* had fully described the methods of geometry and mathematics required to perform this flattening with numerical rigor. These methods, described today as stereographic projection are in effect the theory required to understand fully the use of the astrolabe. As we saw, Hermann of Carinthia translated an Arabic version of Ptolemy's *Planisphaerium* into Latin and dedicated his work in 1143 to Thierry of Chartres.

Consider the keen interest in these texts and technologies in a cultural milieu that fostered and incubated literacy and numeracy like nowhere else in Western Europe at the time. It should come as a surprise to no one that the unique preoccupation of the Chartrians in the cultivation and development of the *quadrivium* stands out in such inordinately abundant imagery in the sculptures of the Royal Portal. There is one complete and one partial Zodiac cycle, a calendar (labors of the months), six or possibly seven astrolabes, an orchestra of musical instruments in the hands of the 24 Elders, images of Pythagoras, Euclid, Ptolemy and Boethius, the geometrical symmetry and proportions of the compositions, the list goes on. The degree of abundance, emphasis and redundancy in the portrayal of these subjects is unique to Chartres; you will find it nowhere else in Gothic monuments. It is a reflection of the Chartrian milieu's keen intellectual focus on the application of concepts of number, order, quantity, and measurement to their knowledge of the world and the Cosmos. I think that in this abundance there is more than enough data or information to trigger in the mind of an astronomically informed observer, the idea of instrument-aided observational astronomy as a legitimate and beneficial pursuit and as a matter of natural philosophy. This connects meaningfully with the sanctification of the Seven Liberal Arts depicted over the Incarnation door. The idea that Chartrian knowledge and teachings of astronomy and cosmology, including precession, are the subject of additional layers of symbolic expression in the sculptures and stained glass of Chartres Cathedral simply cannot be ignored.

More on Precession

I will briefly review the modern astronomical and physical concepts of precession before considering the validity of my hypothesis in more detail and how it provides an improved understanding of the Chartrian Zodiac artwork and its cultural milieu.

In modern astronomy and physics, it is a bit unfortunate that the term precession designates two very different things. In Astronomy general precession is the retrograde displacement of the two equinoctial points in the sky as something observable from the perspective of a person on Earth. In physics, precession designates the gyrating motion of the axis of any spinning body such as a top or a gyroscope or a planet. For the beginner, this can lead to some confusion. While it is true that the physical gyration of the Earth is part of the reason we see a movement of the equinoctial points, this is not the whole story.

A small part of the motion of these two points arises because of the slow wobble of the ecliptic plane. Accordingly, astronomers now speak of the movement of the equinoctial points as general precession, and agree that this motion arises from two separate physical components.[37] Precession of the equator accounts for 50.3 arc seconds per year retrograde. Precession of the ecliptic accounts for 0.1 arc seconds per year prograde. The net effect, the sum of the two motions, is 50.3 arc seconds retrograde.

Figure 22 illustrates the precession of the equator or axial precession, motion due to the physical gyration of the Earth.

The astronomers and philosophers of late antiquity and medieval times understood nothing of the physics and the gravitational effects that shape these motions. Nevertheless, they strove to understand the motions, to measure them, to quantify their rates and to seek models like the armillary sphere and astrolabe to help give a reasoned and quantified understanding of their structure and their behaviour.

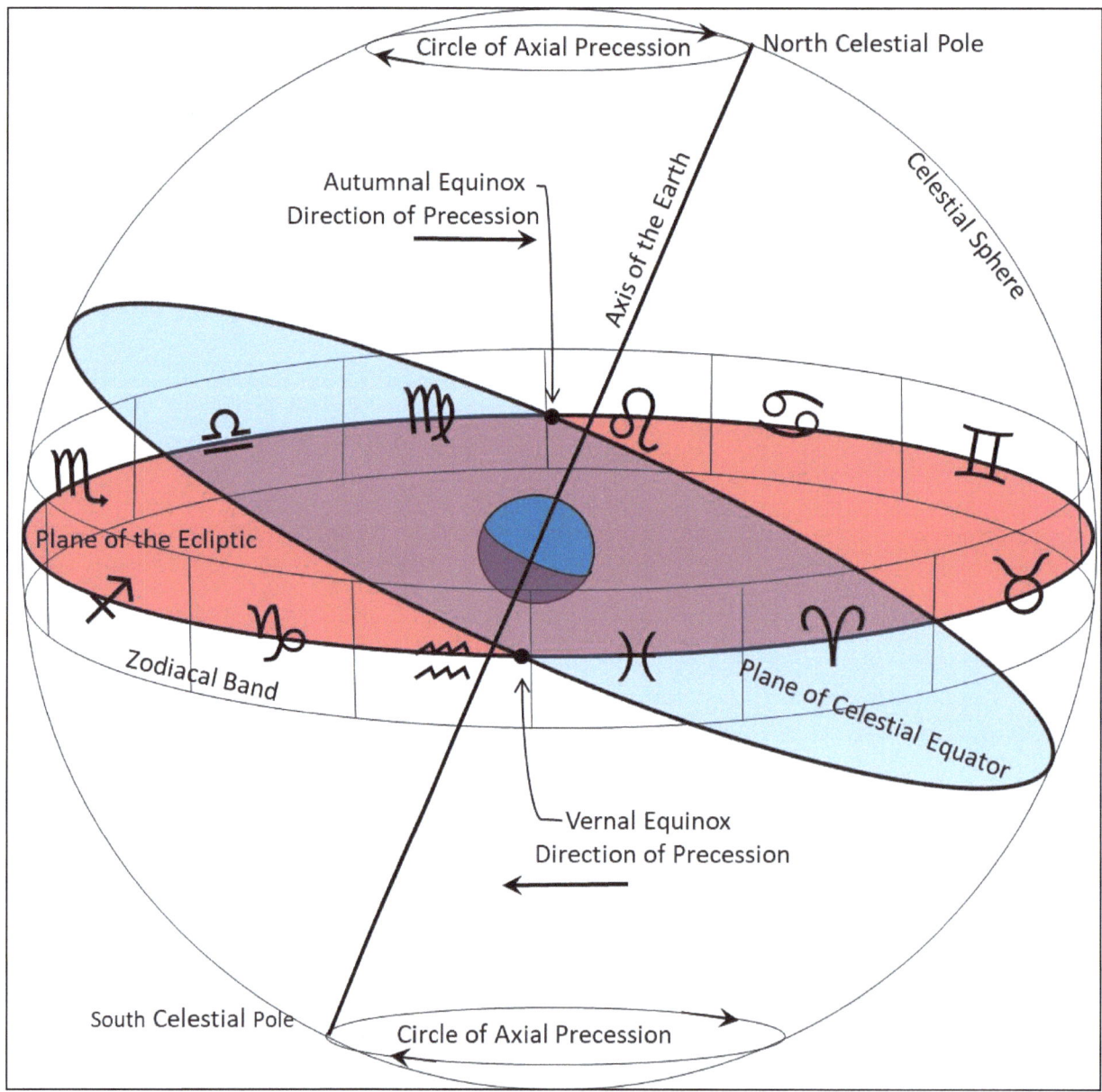

Figure 22 - **Precession of the Equator or Axial Precession** – Earth's equator makes an angle of 23.5 degrees with the ecliptic (the plane of Earth's orbit). Earth gyrates, much like a spinning top or gyroscope and the gyrating axis traces a circle of precession on the celestial sphere, in a retrograde direction. The gyrating equator's points of intersection with the ecliptic also move along retrograde making a complete circle of the ecliptic in about 25,771.6 years.

Image: Legault

Chartres - The Disconnected Zodiac

Challenging the Hypothesis

My hypothesis uses precession to explain the deeper meaning of the Zodiac anomalies as an early instance of a timekeeping method we now call zodiacal or precessional ages, to delineate historical periods and quantify epochs of time. As for any hypothesis, this idea needs to be met with scepticism and challenged. It is important to ask how well it stands up to the rigors of falsifiability and testing against documented facts of medieval history.

There are strong opinions in the literature on the scarcity of primary sources from the late classical and medieval periods that show unequivocally that anybody ever used precessional or zodiacal ages as a timekeeping structure to delineate historical periods or to measure and quantify epochs of time. For instance, Nicholas Campion, a respected cultural historian and specialist in the history of astronomy and astrology, writes:

> In spite of a century of debate about the religious significance of precession, astrologers themselves were slow to incorporate it into their work, and *the earliest known reference to the precessional ages* occurred in the English astrologer AJ Pearce's *The Textbook of Astrology* [1879, my emphasis].[38]

> The use of the precession of the equinoxes as a means of dividing historical epochs has *no basis in astrological tradition prior to the late nineteenth-century* [my emphasis].[39]

> There is though, *not a single extant example of the use of precession of the equinoxes to predict the future by astrologers until the late nineteenth century*. There are indeed arguments that precession was used by astrologers in the ancient world, but they are based entirely on the retrospective interpretation of circumstantial evidence and lack any textual support. […] Literary evidence is not everything but, when it is entirely absent in the works of people who should have been most concerned with it, *the fact does require some attention. Simply, there are no extant classical or medieval astrological texts which attribute any astrological or historical significance to precession* [my emphasis.][40]

On the strength of Campion's research and in the absence of any evidence I can advance to the contrary, I think it is a mistake to project the idea of Zodiacal Ages back in time into medieval minds. The idea of Zodiacal Ages, as we know it today in popular culture and as abused and promoted by tellers of fortunes by Sun Sign Astrology, is a modern invention. The medieval concept of ages of world history, known as the *Six World Ages* was entirely different. They were based on Biblical periods not on astronomical ones. The biblical ages or epochs were described in the late second century by Theophilus of Antioch[41] and further refined by Augustine of Hippo, *circa* 400, in *de catechizandis rudibus* (On the Catechising of the Uninstructed):

> Five ages of the world, accordingly, having been now completed (there has entered the sixth). Of these ages the first is from the beginning of the human race[…] down to Noah, who constructed the ark at the time of the flood. Then the second extends from that period on to Abraham[…].For the third age extends from Abraham on to David the king; the fourth from David on to that captivity whereby the people of God passed over into Babylonia; and the fifth from that transmigration down to the advent of our Lord Jesus Christ. With His coming the sixth age has entered on its process […].
>
> Augustine, *De catechizandis rudibus*[42]

Chartres -The Disconnected Zodiac

Accordingly, I think I need to exclude from my hypothesis any idea that in medieval times there was a well-developed view of world history systematically and chronologically structured along the lines of zodiacal ages. Doing otherwise would be going too far on too little evidence. Nonetheless, I do think it is plausible that the astronomically keen minded Chartrians could quite plausibly have used the idea of precession in a visual metaphor to depict a slice of time corresponding to the Old Testament period, from *Genesis* to the Incarnation. This is the period that for Augustine comprised the first five Biblical ages. Considering the main grouping of Signs in the Royal Portal is structured by season, and reasoning by analogy, the sense I get is that the historical period designated by the disconnected Pisces and Gemini might have been thought of as a cosmic or theological season of a kind. I admit this may sound like splitting hairs and I find my own hypothesis in want of stronger validation based on more solid historical or scientific evidence. I think the hypothesis is valid for two reasons. One is testability; the other is the on-going historical presence and role played by the concept of precession in the medieval quest for more accurate calendar keeping.

Testability

One of the standard approaches to the scientific testing of hypotheses is to try to falsify them by predicting consequences that should become observable only if the hypothesis is correct. On this score, if my hypothesis is correct then further study of the sources for the curriculum of the *quadrivium* at the Cathedral School of Chartres at the time of Thierry should find that knowledge of Al-Battani's book *De motu stellarum* was a source preferred over Ptolemy in the matter of precession. On the contrary, if it becomes evident that some other source was preferred, say Ptolemy or Origen, then that would clearly falsify the hypothesis and justify its rejection. The kind of evidence to look for would be a statement or comment of the kind later made by Copernicus, cited below. Passing this test would by no means prove the hypothesis is correct. However, it would justify retaining it as a tentative explanation, pending further research and the finding of additional corroborating or opposing evidence. Until this test can be performed, I turn my attention to the on-going issue in medieval times of calibrating an accurate calendar.

Calendar Reform and Precession

While Nicholas Campion may be correct about the absence of the treatment of precession in medieval astrological texts, this is certainly not the case in texts and artwork dealing with astronomy and timekeeping.

Chartres - The Disconnected Zodiac

In October 1582, Pope Gregory XIII introduced the Gregorian calendar in the papal bull *Inter gravissimas* (Latin for: Among the Most Serious).[43] By then, the earlier Julian calendar had fallen 10 days out of step, due to precession, with the dates the Council of Nicea had fixed in AD 325 for the equinoxes. The discrepancy arose because precession makes the tropical year shorter than the Julian calendar year by about 11 minutes and 15 seconds. The tropical year, measured from equinox to equinox, is on average 365 days, 5 hours, 48 minutes, 45 seconds or 365.242189 days, in decimal notation. To the nearest second, this is the actual amount of time it takes the Sun to return to the same equinox position and this period tracks the seasons. The Julian calendar year was fixed at exactly 365.25 days, as adopted directly from the Egyptians, whose year was based on the period between heliacal risings of star Sirius (the Sothis cycle). Accordingly, the Julian year was an approximation closer to the true Sidereal Year measured today, from fixed star to fixed star, as 365.256363 days.

Doing the math, in the period of 1,257 years from the Council of Nicea in AD 325 to the calendar reform in AD 1582, the difference of 0.007811 days per year between the Tropical and Julian years accumulates to almost 10 full days (1,257 years x 0.00781 days = 9.818 days).

In 2009 Ari Ben-Menahem, wrote in his *Historical Encyclopedia of Natural and Mathematical Sciences* that the growing calendar discrepancy, caused by precession, had been well known since the early medieval period, specifically by Bede noting a three day error in the 8th century.[44] Later Roger Bacon, *ca.* 1200, noted a seven or eight day error. Later still, Johannes Sacrobosco wrote in his book *De Anni Ratione* (Latin for: On Reckoning the Years), *ca.*1235, that the Julian calendar was out of step with the equinoxes by ten days and that some correction was needed.

By the late Middle Ages, the problem was so ubiquitous that even poets and artists were aware of it. Dante Alighieri, writing *ca.* 1300, drew attention to the issue and the need for calendar reform. In *circa* 1412 the Limbourg Brothers, (Paul, Jean and Herman) began their work on one of the most beautifully illuminated books of hours ever produced: *Les Très Riches Heures du Duc de Berry*. Its calendar illumination and zodiacal diagram for March, shown in Figure 14, for example, shows the cusp between Pisces and Aries, the Vernal Equinox, at 12 March, a full 9 days earlier than the March 21 date that the Council of Nicea had fixed. As Otto Neugebauer comments, *The Très Riches Heures* also records the discrepancy in the table entries for the length of daylight: "The table for the length of daylight provides us also with the dates assumed for the solstices and equinoxes. The entries for 12h [hours of daylight, i.e. the equinoxes] are found at March 12 and September 15."[45]

Chartres - The Disconnected Zodiac

How would historians make sense of historical periods without a reliably calibrated calendar of one kind or another? Considering the size of calendar discrepancies that can accumulate over centuries due to precession, the issue, considered by the likes of Bede, Bacon, Sacrobosco, Alighieri and the Limbourg Brothers, was indeed of rather substantial historical significance. Moreover, when resolution of the issue of calendar reform to correct for precession finally came, it was rather aptly named as 'among the most serious.'

Copernicus, Al-Battani and Precession

The Polish priest and astronomer Nicolaus Copernicus lived on the cusp between the Middle Ages and Modern times, often pegged at the year 1500. He was born in 1473 and died in 1543. In about 1530 he completed his masterwork in six books entitled *De Revolutionibus Orbium Coelestium* (Latin for: On the Revolutions of the Heavenly Spheres). It was not published, however, until 1543. This work shows not only his knowledge of Al-Battani but expresses a preference for Al-Battani's rate of precession over Ptolemy's rate:

> Venus, although bigger than Mercury, can occult barely a hundredth of the sun. So says *Al-Battani of Raqqa*, who thinks that the sun's diameter is ten times larger [than Venus'], and therefore so minute a speck is not easily descried in the most brilliant light [...] I said, however, that the annual revolutions of the center and of inclination are nearly equal. For if they were exactly equal, the equinoctial and solstitial points as well as the entire obliquity of the ecliptic would have to show no shift at all with reference to the sphere of the fixed stars. But since there is a slight variation, *it was discovered only as it grew larger with the passage of time. From Ptolemy to us the precession of the equinoxes amounts to almost 21°.*   Copernicus [my emphasis] [46]

This passage is clear evidence of the use of precession – the displacement of the equinoxes by almost 21° - to measure and quantify a defined historical interval, "from Ptolemy to us." Al-Battani's precession rate of 54.5 arc seconds per year for the 1,362 years between Copernicus' book and the death of Ptolemy in 168 CE gives 20.62 degrees. Ptolemy's much slower rate would give only 13.75 degrees. The preference of Copernicus for Al-Battani is clear. Moreover, the above passage on precession comes at the beginning of the book. He mentions Al-Battani and introduces precession as part of the core evidence that helps prove the Earth revolves around the Sun. In fact, Book III or fully one sixth of the entire work is devoted exclusively to a discussion of precession. Considering this is the book most often credited as terminating the medieval period by triggering the greatest scientific revolution in history, it is difficult to imagine a discussion of precession in a context of greater historical significance.

Chartres - The Disconnected Zodiac

Evidence and Hypothesis Assessed

It is clear that the concept of precession in one form or another was in continuous presence on the minds of Christian thinkers from late antiquity to the end of the middle ages. It was there early on as an argument against astrological fortune telling, later, as a thorny issue of calendrical time keeping, and in the end as evidence of Earth's orbital motion around the Sun. Copernicus clearly expected his medieval minded audience to understand, without any explanatory elaboration, that a 20 degree precession of the equinoxes, at Al-Battani's rate, could delineate a 1,362 year period of time, of history. Moreover, he could do this without invoking anything like the modern concept of zodiacal ages, which, at any rate had not yet been invented. Accordingly, there is absolutely nothing that precludes his predecessors in the mid-twelfth century Chartrian community from having done exactly the same thing to delineate the duration of the Old Testament period. I suggest that this is exactly the deeper meaning of the zodiac anomalies of Chartres Cathedral. Moreover, the suggestion rises above the status of mere guesswork or conjecture. It qualifies as a valid scientific hypothesis because it is testable and could easily be falsified by the right kind of evidence.

Chartres - The Disconnected Zodiac

6. BACK TO THE WINDOW

The Gemini-Taurus Transposition

And lastly, why do I think the Gemini-Taurus transposition in the Chartres' Zodiac Window was deliberate? My answer is really quite simple. Once he set aside Ptolemy's rate of precession in favour of Al-Battani's, it made sense for a Chartrian to also set aside Taurus in favour of Gemini because now he knew Gemini was a marker for the beginning of time. He now knew he could numerically map the moment God created the Cosmos, the Alpha moment of Christian time, onto a point early, or at the feet, so to speak, of Gemini.

According to Merlet and Clerval, the image for May preferred at Chartres and elsewhere, is usually a hunter with a horse:

> *A Chartres, dans les zodiaques sculptés de la Cathédrale, comme d'ailleurs dans la plupart des autres calendriers, le chasseur à cheval symbolise le mois de mai.* (At Chartres, in the zodiac sculptures of the Cathedral, as, in any case, in the majority of other calendars, a hunter on horseback symbolizes the month of May [my translation]). [47]

This description accords well with the Royal Portal sculpture for May, shown in Figure 4 - a bearded man in simple attire, wearing gloves and a cape with horse and falcon that looks very much like a hunter. It also accords well with the description recorded by Etienne Houvet.[48] In the North Porch archivolt, the image for May is also a hunter. Even though he is beardless and on foot without a horse, he is identified clearly by the attribute of a hunter's falcon, as seen in Figure 23.

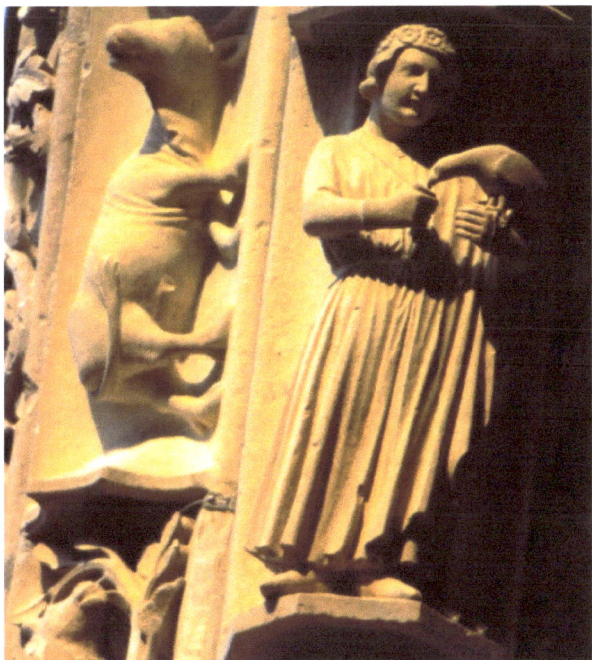

Figure 23 – May-Taurus in the North Porch archivolts of Chartres Cathedral, ca. 1215. Image University of Pittsburgh, see:
https://digital.library.pitt.edu/islandora/object/pitt%3AFCSP22815100/viewer

Chartres - The Disconnected Zodiac

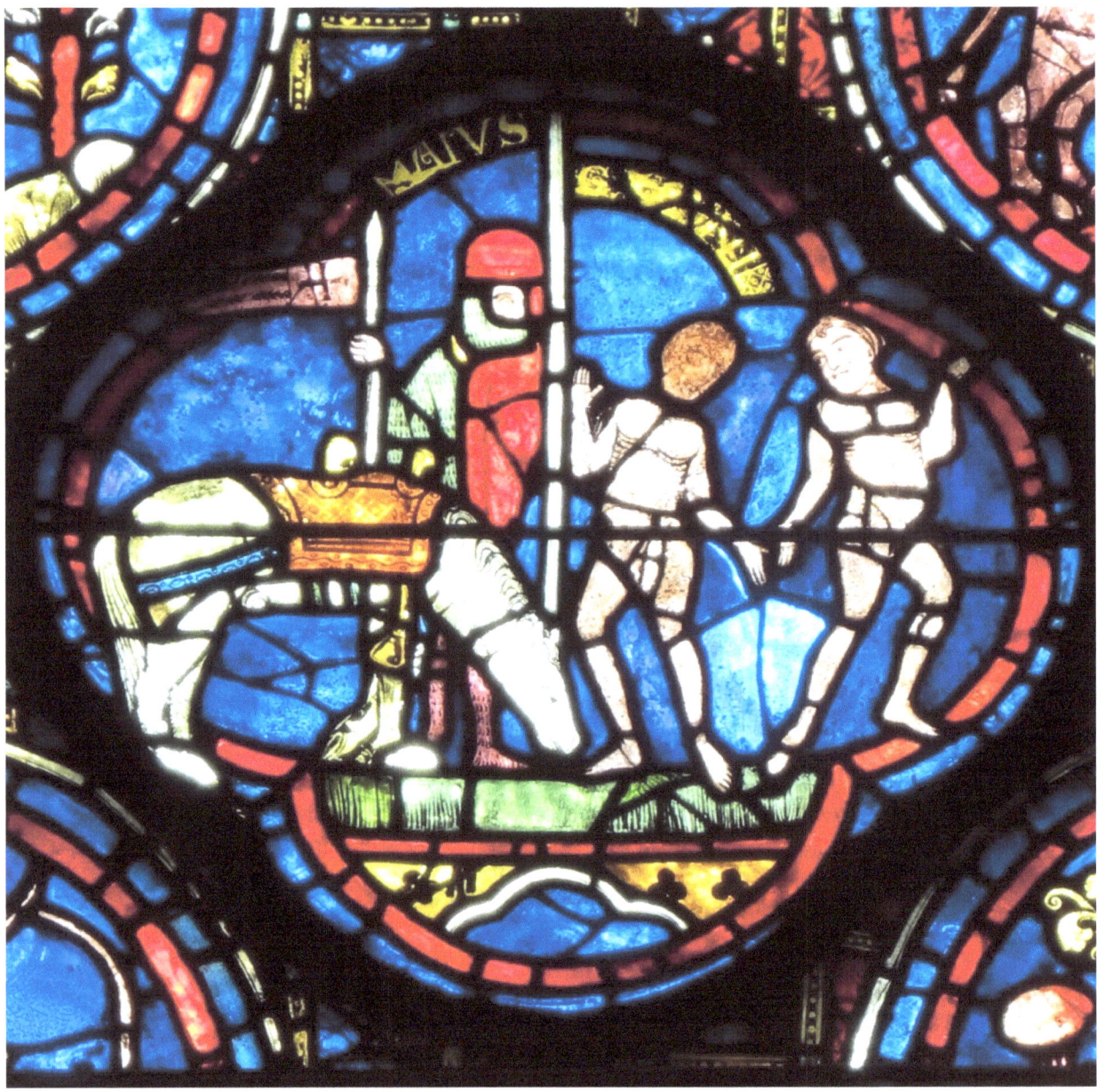

Figure 24 - The May / Gemini Pane in the Chartres Zodiac Window, *ca.* 1217. Image cropped from: https://upload.wikimedia.org/wikipedia/commons/c/ca/Chartres-028-g_composite.jpg

Consider now the May/Gemini pane in the Zodiac Window, shown in Figure 24. What are we to make of an equestrian in full chainmail armour, complete with helmet, shield, lance, flag and saddled horse? Is this the attire and equipment of a hunter or of an armoured and combat ready cavalryman? Moreover, if any hunting at all was going on in an earlier moment, something has interrupted it because the cavalryman has dismounted and placed his lance at rest while guardedly holding his shield close to his

Chartres -The Disconnected Zodiac

chest. Rather than stalk game, he gazes wide eyed in rapt attention at a white pole standing against a blue sky, planted vertically upon the horizon line. This white pole splits the scene vertically in half. The horse and cavalryman stand on one side in the earthly realm and the Gemini Twins, on the other side, in the heavenly realm. The white pole intersects at 90 degrees a black line that cuts dead centre horizontally through the scene. The black line is the metal armature of the window pane and, like a virtual equator, it divides the entire pane into equal upper and lower halves.

The cavalryman's mount has found something worth munching, lower down, near the point where the pole stands on the horizon. Moreover, the breeching strap girding the mount's haunches is the only element in the image that is the same blue as the sky. The sky-blue strap is adorned with equally spaced segments and it intersects the black 'equator' line of the armature at what looks to be very close to a 23.5 degree angle. The placement of these two lines at such an angle, the segmentation on the strap and its placement on the very spherical hindquarter of the horse are elements very suggestive to me of armillary sphere imagery. Could the angle of the armature and strap in this windowpane somehow allude to the intersection of the equator with the ecliptic?

The Gemini Twins, standing in the heavenly realm, both gesture with their hands in a downward direction toward their feet. The horse's nose pokes past the pole that separates the two realms, and it is very interested in something just inside the heavenly realm, at the feet of Gemini. Accordingly, I sense the glazier is using the body language of the horse and the twins to direct my attention to something important lower, or rather, earlier, at the feet, so to speak, of Gemini. Could the downward gesturing of the horse and the Twins symbolically indicate an earlier place of the equinoctial intersection point at the feet of Gemini? This question connects meaningfully with the inordinately large shield in the Royal Portal sculpture of Gemini, in Figure 4 that also seems to point to something of exceptional importance at the prominently visible feet of Gemini. The tapering shield guides the eye downward toward the feet of the Twins. As seen in Figure 17, the toes of the Twins and tip of the shield eye-catchingly protrude beyond the edge of the pedestal on which they stand.

As for the military equestrian garb of our supposed hunter, is it just a coincidence that *equites*, the Latin word for 'cavalry' sounds almost exactly like *equitas*, the Latin word for 'equality' that shares its root prefix with 'equinox' and 'equator'?

Perhaps I let this fanciful imagery persuade me too easily. Perhaps my sense of skepticism is too lax. Be that as it may, I cannot help but to sense, in spite of a 72-year gap between the sculpture and the glass, an eloquently subtle allusion in these images that connect meaningfully with the placement of the equinox at the feet of Gemini.

Chartres - The Disconnected Zodiac

Moreover, it is because of the redundancy of emphasis on the Feet of Gemini, seen in both the sculptures and the glass, that it becomes evident to me that the transposition in the window and the disconnected placement in the sculpture are deliberate. The unconventional structure of the Signs and Months in the sculptures represent seasonal intervals of time. The four terminal points that designate the end points of the seasons – the equinoxes and solstices – are all positioned together at the top of the archivolt, centred on the mutilated remnant of a dove in the keystone. I think the decision to pair Gemini with Pisces, instead of with their months, must also point, by analogy, to an interval of time, an interval or a season of much greater duration and of much greater significance to Christianity than the simple seasons of the earthly year. It points to the cosmic interval between Creation and Incarnation, the interval between the Alpha point and the intermediate point, two of the three fundamental points in the Christian concept of finite time.

Proof and Understanding

You can take an image of a circle and prove, with absolute certainty, using geometry and algebra, that the area is exactly equal to π times the square of the radius. But where, pray tell, is the exactitude of geometry and algebra that proves how the exact same circle may be used, say, as a nimbus to convey a theological concept such as sainthood? No evidence short of an explicit comment by the original artist(s) can ever be sufficient to prove with absolute certainty that my reading of the zodiac anomalies of Chartres is correct. The symbolic meaning of images is always only something you can understand, not prove. Accordingly, I must let my reading of the Disconnected Zodiac rest as a hypothesis, at best.

The Mathesis Connection

However interesting my hypothesis may be and however much fun you can have playing around with and connecting medieval dots between calendars, astronomy, geometry and wordplay, I really think, that there is a much more serious historical connection to be made in all of this business.

I have grounded my hypothesis that explains the highly unusual ordering and discontinuity of the Royal Portal Zodiac, on the astronomy of precession, on numerically measured time keeping and on the keen interest of the Chartrians in the business of applying numbers – the teachings of the *quadrivium* - to theology and to natural philosophy. We know how keen they were to do this from the books they kept and the books they wrote. Chartres Cathedral itself is one of these books. We need to

Chartres - The Disconnected Zodiac

make a more serious effort to relearn how to read it. I feel so strongly about this point that I include the Cathedral as an entry in the Reference section of this booklet, under the authorship of Thierry de Chartres *et al*.

Today, it is the word *mathesis* that designates the agenda, to call it that, of 'numerizing' or mathematicising knowledge. It is derived from the Greek μάθησις, *mathesis* 'science or learning'. It appears primarily in philosophical discussions of the historical quest for a *scientia mathematica universalis* or a universal science grounded in mathematics. The historical outline of this quest usually starts with an initial nod to Pythagoras, Plato, and their followers. Generally ignoring the Middle Ages altogether, it then jumps straight to the Italian renaissance with the work of Marsilio Ficino and Galileo, in a rush to get to Descartes, Leibniz and then to perhaps the greatest work of mathesis of all time, Newton's *Principia*. Its full title is *Philosophiæ Naturalis Principia Mathematica*, Latin for 'Mathematical Principles of Natural Philosophy.'

Make no mistake: it is to a long and multi-generational journey of mathesis that we owe the debt of developing what the Chartrians knew as Natural Philosophy into what we know today as Astronomy, Cosmology, Physics and Science. To overlook their role on that long and arduous journey through time would leave too many dots disconnected.

Richard J Legault is a free-lance journalist. Some of his work has appeared in the journal *Caerdroia* and in the *Journal of the Royal Astronomical Society of Canada*. He lives in Ottawa.
richardjlegault@gmail.com.

Last Updated: 20 April 2022

Chartres -The Disconnected Zodiac

REFERENCES

Augustine of Hippo **circa** 400 *On the Catechising of the Uninstructed* Trans. S. D. F. Salmond CreateSpace Independent Publishing Platform, 2015, ISBN-10 : 1514266636, ISBN-13 : 978-1514266632, Page 84, digital version consulted 14 April 2021 at URL: https://ccel.org/ccel/schaff/npnf103/npnf103.iv.iii.xxiii.html

Ball, Philip 2008 *Universe of Stone: Chartres Cathedral and the Triumph of the Medieval Mind* Bodley Head, London.

Bede (the Venerable) and Wallis, F. (ed.) 1999 *Bede, The Reckoning of Time* Liverpool University Press ISBN: 9780853236931.

Ben-Menahem, Ari 2009 *Historical Encyclopedia of Natural and Mathematical Sciences* Springer, New York. Consulted 31 May 2017 at URL: https://books.google.ca/books?redir_esc=y&id=9tUrarQYhKMC&q=precession#v=snippet&q=calendar&f=false

Bishop, Roy L. and Turner, David G 2016 "Astronomical Precession" in *Observer's Handbook 2017*, James S. Edgar, Editor, Royal Astronomical Society of Canada, Toronto 2016.

Bugslag, James 2017 **Chartres – Zodiac Cycle**, private correspondence.

Burnett, Charles S. F. 1978 "Arabic into Latin in Twelfth-Century Spain: the Works of Hermann of Carinthia", in *Mittellateinisches Jahrbuch*, 13, 1978, pp. 100–134. Consulted 26 April 2017 at URL: http://www.mgh-bibliothek.de/dokumente/a/a053253.pdf

Campion, Nicholas 2012 *Astrology and Popular Religion in the Modern West: Prophecy, Cosmology and the New Age* page 22 Ashgate.

Clavius, Christoph 1603 *Romani Calendarii A Gregorio XIII. P. M. restitvti explicatio S. D. N. Clementis VIII. P. M. Ivssv edita : accesit confutatio eorum, qui Calendarium aliter instaurandum esse contenderunt* [],Rome, Zannetti. The papal bull Inter gravissimas issued by Pope Gregory XIII on February 24, 1582 begins on page 53, counting from the front cover. The title page is page 5. Digital copy consulted 11 March 2020 at URL: http://echo.mpiwg-berlin.mpg.de/ECHOdocuView?url=/mpiwg/online/permanent/library/YXK9FE9W/pageimg&start=51&viewMode=images&mode=imagepath&pn–53&ww=0.2603&wh−0.2603&wx=0.0694&wy=0.2921&ws=3

Copernicus, Nicolaus 1543 *De Revolutionibus Orbium Coelestium*, [On the Revolutions of the Heavenly Spheres] translator Charles Glen Wallis, in Hawking 2002.

Crummy, Nina 2005 "From bracelets to battle-honours: military armillae from the Roman conquest of Britain" in N. Crummy (ed.), Image, *Craft and the Classical World. Essays in honour of Donald Bailey and Catherine Johns* (Monogr. Instrumentum 29), Montagnac 2005, pp. 93-105.

Chartres - The Disconnected Zodiac

Delporte, Eugène Joseph and International Astronomical Union 1930 *Délimitation scientifique des constellations (tables et cartes)* [Scientific delimitation of the constellations (Tables and Charts)] At the University Press, Cambridge.

Delporte, Eugène Joseph and International Astronomical Union 1930 *Atlas céleste* [Celestial Atlas] At the University Press, Cambridge

Dronke, Peter ed. 1978 *Bernard Silvestris Cosmographia* Brill, Leiden.

Durand, Paul 1881 *Monographie de Notre-Dame de Chartres: Explication des planches*, Imprimerie Nationale, Paris. A digital copy at: https://archive.org/details/monographiedenot00durauoft/page/45/mode/1up.

Edgar, James ed. 2016 *Observer's Handbook 2017*, The Royal Astronomical Society of Canada, Toronto, Ontario.

Ellard, Peter 2007 *The Sacred Cosmos–Theological, Philosophical and Scientific Conversations in the Twelfth Century School of Chartres*, University of Scranton Press, Chicago Illinois.

Evans, James and Berggren, J. L. *Geminos's Introduction to the Phenomena: A Translation and Study of a Hellenistic Survey of Astronomy* Princeton University Press, 2006.

Fassler, Margot E. 2010 *The Virgin of Chartres – Making History through Liturgy and the Arts* Yale University Press, New Haven.

Fassler, Margot Elsbeth 1993 "Liturgy and Sacred History in the Twelfth-Century Tympana at Chartres" in *The Art Bulletin* Vol. 75, No. 3, Sep., 1993.

Harmer, John Reginald (ed.) Lightfoot, Joseph Barber (trans.) *The Apostolic Fathers:* Macmillan, 1891. Digital copy consulted 22 July 2021 at URL: https://books.google.ca/books?id=pcIyAQAAMAAJ&printsec=frontcover#v=onepage&q&f=false

Hawking, Stephen 2002 *On the Shoulders of Giants – The Great Works of Physics and Astronomy* Running Press Philadelphia, Pennsylvania.

Hermann of Carinthia 1143 *Preface of the Planisphere of Claudius Ptolemy* in Burnet 1978.

Holmes, C. N "The Zodiac" in *Popular Astronomy*, vol. 22, pp.547-550, digital copy consulted on 20 July 2021 at URL: http://articles.adsabs.harvard.edu//full/1914PA.....22..547H/0000547.000.html

Hourihane, Colum, 2007 *Time in the Medieval World: Occupations of the Months and Signs of the Zodiac in the Index of Christian Art*, ISBN 9780976820222 Princeton University.

IAU (International Astronomical Union) "The Constellations" on the IAU web site consulted 3 March 2020 at URL: https://www.iau.org/public/themes/constellations/

James, John 2009: *In Search of the Unknown in Medieval Architecture* Pindar Press, New York.

Ignatius of Antioch to Polycarp in Harmer 1891.

Chartres -The Disconnected Zodiac

Katzenellenbogen, Adolf 1964 *The Sculptural Programs of Chartres Cathedral* W. W. Norton & Co, New York. https://archive.org/details/sculpturalprogra0000katz

Knitter, Brian John 2000 "Thierry of Chartres and the West Façade Sculpture of Chartres Cathedral" San Jose State University Master's Theses, Paper 2052.

Legault, Richard J 2021 'Chartres Royal Portal – Icons for All Seasons' monograph work –in-progress posted at URL:
https://www.academia.edu/40100368/Chartres_Royal_Portal_Icons_for_All_Seasons

Lévis-Godechot, Nicole 1987 *Chartres révélée par sa sculpture et ses vitraux* (Chartres revealed by her sculpture and her stained glass windows) Zodiaque, Paris

Lewis, George 1911 *The Philocalia of Origen – A Compilation of Selected Passages from Origen's Works made by Gregory of Nazianzus and Basil of Caesarea* T & T Clark, Edingurgh 1911. Digital copy consulted 22 July, 2021 at URL:
https://archive.org/details/philocaliaoforig00orig/page/190/mode/2up?q=zodiac

Mâle, Emile 1958 *The Gothic Image: Religious Art in France of the 13th Century,* translated by Dora Nussey, Harper & Row, New York.

Mâle, Emile 1983 *Chartres* Harper and Row, New York.

Maxfield, Valerie A. 1981 *The Military Decorations of the Roman Army*, pp. 89-91. University of California Press: Berkeley and Los Angeles;

Merlet, René and Clerval, Alexandre 1893 *Un manuscrit chartrain du XIe siècle* [A Chartrian Manuscript of the 11th Century] Garnier. Digital copy consulted 4 March 2020 at URL:
https://archive.org/details/unmanuscritchart00merl/page/n15/mode/2up

Minio-Paluello "Plato of Tivoli" *Complete Dictionary of Scientific Biography* 2008, cited by Encyclopedia.com retrieved 29 Oct. 2013 from URL:
https://www.encyclopedia.com/science/dictionaries-thesauruses-pictures-and-press-releases/plato-tivoli

Morey, Charles R. 1912 "The Origin of the Fish Symbol" in *The Princeton Theological Review* Volume 10 issue 2 Pages 278-298 (21 pages).

Neugebauer O. 1983 'Appendix C: Astronomical and Calendrical Data in the Tres Riches Heures' in: *Astronomy and History Selected Essays*. Springer, New York, NY.
https://doi.org/10.1007/978-1-4612-5559-8_41

National Aeronautics and Space Administration *Dictionary of Technical Terms for Aerospace Use. NASA SP-7*, edited by William H. Allen, 314 pages, published by NASA, Washington, D.C., 1965, web site consulted 12 June 2021 at URL:
https://er.jsc.nasa.gov/seh/g.html

O'Connor, John J.; Robertson, Edmund F., 1999 "Abu Abdallah Mohammad ibn Jabir Al-Battani", in *MacTutor History of Mathematics archive*, University of St Andrews, retrieved 29 October 2013 from:

Chartres -The Disconnected Zodiac

http://www-history.mcs.st-andrews.ac.uk/Biographies/Al-Battani.html

Origen *ca.* 250 *Philocalia* in Lewis 1911.

Plato, *Timaeus*, cited in Ellard 2007.

Rasimus, Tuomas 2012 "Revisiting the Ichthys: A Suggestion Concerning the Origins of Christological Fish Symbolism" in *Mystery and Secrecy in the Nag Hammadi Collection and Other Ancient Literature: Ideas and Practices*, edited by Christian Bull, Liv Ingeborg Lied and John Turner. NHMS 76. Leiden: Brill Pp. 327–348.

Schaff, Philip 2004 *Fathers of the Second Century: Hermas, Tatian, Athenagoras, Theophilus, and Clement of Alexandria (Entire)* Grand Rapids, MI: Christian Classics Ethereal Library 2004. Digital copy consulted 13 July 2021 at URL:
https://www.documentacatholicaomnia.eu/03d/1819-1893,_Schaff._Philip,_1_Vol_02_Fathers_Of_The_Second_Century,_EN.pdf

Silvestris, Bernardus 1147 *Cosmographia* cited in Dronke 1978.

Theophilus of Antioch 169 *Apologia ad Autolycum*, Book III Chapter 28, in Schaff 2004.

Thierry de Chartres *et al. La Cathédrale Notre-Dame de Chartres* (Our Lady of Chartres Cathedral), lithoscript monument, Cathedral School of Chartres, Chartres, in phases from *circa* 1145 to *circa* 1219.

Truitt, Elly R. "Celestial Divination and Arabic Science in Twelfth-Century England: The History of Gerbert of Aurillac's Talking Head." In *the Journal of the History of Ideas* 73, no. 2 (2012): 201-222. PDF Version at URL:
https://repository.brynmawr.edu/cgi/viewcontent.cgi?article=1012&context=history_pubs

Van Der Meulen, Jan and Price, Nancy Waterman 1981 *The West Portals of Chartres Cathedral Volume 1- The Iconology of the Creation* University Press of America.

Chartres - The Disconnected Zodiac

NOTES

1 **Houvet,** Étienne, 1919 *Cathédrale de Chartres; portail occidental ou royal, XIIe siècle* Chelles, Imp. A. Faucheux, consulted 10 August 2019 at URL: https://archive.org/details/cathdraledecha00houv

2 **Hourihane,** Colum, 2007 *Time in the Medieval World: Occupations of the Months and Signs of the Zodiac in the Index of Christian Art*, ISBN 9780976820222 Princeton University.

3 **Ellard**, Peter 2007 *The Sacred Cosmos–Theological, Philosophical and Scientific Conversations in the Twelfth Century School of Chartres*, University of Scranton Press, Chicago Illinois.

4 **Evans**, James and Berggren, J. L. *Geminos's Introduction to the Phenomena: A Translation and Study of a Hellenistic Survey of Astronomy* page 93, Princeton University Press, 2006.

5 **Holmes**, C. N "The Zodiac" in *Popular Astronomy*, 1914 vol. 22, pp.547-550, digital copy consulted on 20 July 2021 at URL: http://articles.adsabs.harvard.edu//full/1914PA.....22..547H/0000547.000.html

6 **IAU** (International Astronomical Union) "The Constellations" on the IAU web site consulted 3 March 2020 at URL: https://www.iau.org/public/themes/constellations/

7 **Delporte**, Eugène Joseph and International Astronomical Union 1930 *Délimitation scientifique des constellations (tables et cartes)* At the University Press, Cambridge; and Delporte, Eugène Joseph and International Astronomical Union 1930 *Atlas céleste* At the University Press, Cambridge.

8 **Plato**, *The Timaeus*, cited in Ellard 2007.

9 **Van Der Meulen,** Jan and Price, Nancy Waterman 1981 *The West Portals of Chartres Cathedral Volume 1- The Iconology of the Creation* University Press of America. See also discussion in Fassler, Margot 1993 "Liturgy and Sacred History in the Twelfth-Century Tympana at Chartres" in *The Art Bulletin* Vol. 75, No. 3, Sep., 1993.

10 **Durand**, Paul 1881 *Monographie de Notre-Dame de Chartres: Explication des planches*, Imprimerie Nationale, Paris, p.45, as cited in Fassler 1993, page 503, footnote 57. A digital copy of Durand's book is preserved at: https://archive.org/details/monographiedenot00durauoft/page/45/mode/1up

11 **Katzenellenbogen**, Adolf 1964 *The Sculptural Programs of Chartres Cathedral*, W. W. Norton & Co, New York, page 20. https://archive.org/details/sculpturalprogra0000katz

12 **James**, John 1974 "Medieval Astrology: the signs of the Zodiac on the Royal Portal of Chartres cathedral", in *The Federation of Australian Astrologers Journal,* iv 1974, 10-13 and v 1975, 7-12, reformatted digital copy consulted 11 March 2020 at URL: https://learnaboutastrology.tumblr.com/post/85406514643/signs-of-the-zodiac-on-the-royal-portal-

63

chartres

13 **Ball**, Philip 2008 *Universe of Stone: Chartres Cathedral and the Triumph of the Medieval Mind* Bodley Head, London, 2008, page 103.

14 **Fassler**, Margot Elsbeth 2010 *The Virgin of Chartres: Making History through Liturgy and the Arts,* p.238, Yale University Press.

15 **Fassler** 2010.

16 **Hourihane** 2007.

17 **Hourihane** 2007, pages lix to lxii.

18 **Hourihane** 2007 page lxix.

19 **Katzenellenbogen** 1964, page 114, note 88.

20 **Merlet**, René and Clerval, Alexandre 1893 *Un manuscrit chartrain du XIe siècle* (A Chartrian Manuscript of the 11th Century) Garnier.
https://archive.org/details/unmanuscritchart00merl/page/14/mode/1up

21 **Morey**, Charles R. 1912 "The Origin of the Fish Symbol" in *The Princeton Theological Review* Volume 10 issue 2 Pages 278-298 (21 pages).

22 **Rasimus,** Tuomas 2012 "Revisiting the Ichthys: A Suggestion Concerning the Origins of Christological Fish Symbolism" in *Mystery and Secrecy in the Nag Hammadi Collection and Other Ancient Literature: Ideas and Practices,* edited by Christian Bull, Liv Ingeborg Lied and John Turner. NHMS 76. Leiden: Brill Pp. 327–348.

23 **Harmer**, John Reginald (ed.) Lightfoot, Joseph Barber (trans.) *The Apostolic Fathers:* Macmillan, 1891, page 161, Digital copy consulted 22 July 2021 at URL:
https://books.google.ca/books?id=pcIyAQAAMAAJ&printsec=frontcover#v=onepage&q&f=false

24 **Theophilus** of Antioch *Apologia ad Autolycum*, Book III Chapter 28, in Schaff, Philip *Fathers of the Second Century: Hermas, Tatian, Athenagoras, Theophilus, and Clement of Alexandria (Entire)* Grand Rapids, MI: Christian Classics Ethereal Library 2004, page 169. Digital copy consulted 13 July 2021 at URL:
https://www.documentacatholicaomnia.eu/03d/1819-1893,_Schaff._Philip,_1_Vol_02_Fathers_Of_The_Second_Century,_EN.pdf

25 **Knitter**, Brian John, "Thierry of Chartres and the west façade sculpture of Chartres Cathedral" (2000). Master's Theses number 2052, page 63.
https://scholarworks.sjsu.edu/cgi/viewcontent.cgi?article=3048&context=etd_theses

26 **Edgar,** James ed. 2017 *Observer's Handbook 2018*, The Royal Astronomical Society of Canada, Toronto,

Ontario, page 21.

27 **National Aeronautics and Space Administration** *Dictionary of Technical Terms for Aerospace Use. NASA SP-7*, edited by William H. Allen, 314 pages, published by NASA, Washington, D.C., 1965, web site consulted 12 June 2021 at URL: https://er.jsc.nasa.gov/seh/g.html

28 **Lewis**, George 1911 *The Philocalia of Origen – A Compilation of Selected Passages from Origen's Works made by Gregory of Nazianzus and Basil of Caesarea*, T&T Clark, Edinburgh 1911, page 191. Digital copy consulted 22 July 2021 at URL:
https://archive.org/details/philocaliaoforig00orig/page/190/mode/2up?q=zodiac

29 **O'Connor**, John J.; Robertson, Edmund F., 1999 "Muhammad ibn Jābir al-Harrānī al-Battānī", in *MacTutor History of Mathematics archive*, University of St Andrews, retrieved 29 October 2013 from:
http://www-history.mcs.st-andrews.ac.uk/Biographies/Al-Battani.html

30 **Minio-Paluello**, Lorenzo 2013 "Plato of Tivoli" in *Complete Dictionary of Scientific Biography* 2008, cited in *Encyclopedia.com*, retrieved 29 Oct. 2013 http://www.encyclopedia.com/doc/1G2-2830903444.html

31 **Burnett**, Charles S. F. 1978 "Arabic into Latin in Twelfth-Century Spain: the Works of Hermann of Carinthia", in *Mittellateinisches Jahrbuch*, 13, 1978, pp. 100–34.

32 **Burnett** 1978, pages 110 and 111.

33 **Ellard** 2007

34 **Lévis-Godechot**, Nicole 1987 *Chartres révélée par sa sculpture et ses vitraux* (Chartres revealed by her sculpture and her stained glass windows) Zodiaque, Paris

35 **Dronke**, Peter ed. 1978 *Bernard Silvestris Cosmographia* Brill, Leiden.

36 **Maxfield**, Valerie A. 1981 *The Military Decorations of the Roman Army*, pp. 89-91. University of California Press: Berkeley and Los Angeles; **Crummy**, Nina 2005 "From bracelets to battle-honours: military armillae from the Roman conquest of Britain" in N. Crummy (ed.), *Image, Craft and the Classical World. Essays in honour of Donald Bailey and Catherine Johns* (Monogr. Instrumentum 29), Montagnac 2005, pp. 93-105

37 **International Astronomer's Union** *2006 Resolution B1*, English version
https://www.iau.org/static/resolutions/IAU2006_Resol1.pdf

38 **Campion**, Nichoas (2004) *Prophecy, cosmology and the New Age movement: the extent and nature of contemporary belief in astrology.* PhD thesis, Bath Spa University. page 59,
http://researchspace.bathspa.ac.uk/1453/1/Nicholas%20Campion%20-%202004.pdf

39 Ibid page 67.

40 **Campion**, Nicholas 2012 *Astrology and Popular Religion in the Modern West: Prophecy, Cosmology and the New Age* Ashgate, page 22.

41 **Theophilus** of Antioch, *op. cit.*

42 **Augustine of Hippo** *circa* 400 *On the Catechising of the Uninstructed* Trans. S. D. F. Salmond CreateSpace Independent Publishing Platform, 2015, ISBN-10 : 1514266636, ISBN-13 : 978-1514266632, Page 84, digital version consulted 14 April 2021 at URL:
https://ccel.org/ccel/schaff/npnf103/npnf103.iv.iii.xxiii.html

43 **Clavius**, Christoph 1603 *Romani Calendarii A Gregorio* XIII. Rome, Zannetti. In the digital copy consulted 14 April 2021, the bull starts on page 53 counting from the front cover. See:
https://echo.mpiwg-berlin.mpg.de/ECHOdocuView?start=51&viewMode=images&mode=imagepath&url=/mpiwg/online/permanent/library/YXK9FE9W/pageimg&pn=55&ws=3

44 **Ben-Menahem,** Ari 2009 *Historical Encyclopedia of Natural and Mathematical Sciences* page 863, Springer, New York.

45 **Neugebauer** O. (1983) 'Appendix C: Astronomical and Calendrical Data' in the *Tres Riches Heures*. In: *Astronomy and History Selected Essays.* Springer, New York, NY. https://doi.org/10.1007/978-1-4612-5559-8_41

46 **Copernicus,** Nicolaus 1543 *De Revolutionibus Orbium Coelestium*, (On the Revolutions of the Heavenly Spheres) translator Charles Glen Wallis, in Hawking 2002.

47 **Merlet**, René and Clerval, Alexandre 1893 *Un manuscrit chartrain du XIe siècle* [A Chartrian Manuscript of the 11th Century] Garnier, on page 12 of the digital PDF copy consulted 4 March 2020 at URL:
https://archive.org/details/unmanuscritchart00merl/page/n15/mode/2up

48 **Houvet** 1919

www.ingramcontent.com/pod-product-compliance
Lightning Source LLC
Chambersburg PA
CBHW051200220526
45473CB00003B/850